AFRICAN AMERICANS OF MARTHA'S VINEYARD

AFRICAN AMERICANS OF

MARTHA'S VINEYARD

From Enslavement to Presidential Visit

THOMAS DRESSER

THE
History
PRESS

Published by The History Press
Charleston, SC 29403
www.historypress.net

Front cover: *top*: Reverend Oscar Denniston and family, *courtesy of the Martha's Vineyard Museum and Doris Clark*; *bottom*: Gay Head cliffs, *photo by Joyce Dresser*.
Back cover: *top*: Birthday party at the home of Dorothy West, *courtesy of Olive Bowles Tomlinson*; *bottom*: The president and family at the Gay Head lighthouse, *courtesy of Tom Wallace, Wallace & Co., Sotheby's International Realty*.

First published 2010
Second printing 2010
Third printing 2011
Fourth printing 2012
Fifth printing 2012

Manufactured in the United States
ISBN 978.1.59629.069.3

Library of Congress Cataloging-in-Publication Data
Dresser, Tom.
African Americans of Martha's Vineyard : from enslavement to presidential visit /
Thomas Dresser.
p. cm.
Includes bibliographical references.
ISBN 978-1-59629-069-3
1. African Americans--Massachusetts--Martha's Vineyard--History. 2. African Americans--Massachusetts--Martha's Vineyard--Biography. 3. Martha's Vineyard (Mass.)--Race relations. 4. Martha's Vineyard (Mass.)--History. 5. Martha's Vineyard (Mass.)--Biography.
I. Title.
F72.M5D74 2010
305.896'07304494--dc22
2010019893

To my grandchildren
Besides time with my wife Joyce—and writing—my favorite time is spent with
my grandchildren: Shealyn, Molly and Dylan.

CONTENTS

Preface   9

Prologue   11

Acknowledgements   13

Chapter 1. Chattel   15

Chapter 2. Abolition   25

Chapter 3. Fugitive   36

Chapter 4. Emancipation   45

Chapter 5. Pacesetters   58

Chapter 6. Promise and Prejudice   74

Chapter 7. Civil Rights   88

Chapter 8. Social Activists   99

Chapter 9. Friends and Family   107

Chapter 10. Heritage Trail   119

Chapter 11. Mr. President   127

Chapter 12. Prominent People   134

Epilogue   147

Notes   151

Bibliography   157

About the Author   159

PREFACE

When President Obama vacationed on the Vineyard in late summer 2009, he added another chapter[1] to the African American experience on Martha's Vineyard. The saga from slavery to emancipation to reconstruction and on through civil rights has been a tortuous struggle, embedded in our national conscience. That the first African American president chose to visit Martha's Vineyard is worthy of inclusion in the heritage of the Vineyard. It was his visit that initiated my intent to write this book.

One may ask what right or experience does a white man have to author a book about African Americans. Good point. I offer an objective account, one step removed, but able to present a perspective that encompasses the story through a wider lens, capturing historical relevance but omitting anger or bias that may taint my tale.

This book is not a memoir. It is not a textbook, nor a litany of ills. Rather, I sought to recount historical events within the timeline of American history. I was daunted, at first, by the task of interviewing African Americans about their Vineyard experiences. However, the outpouring of support, as well as curiosity, has served me well. This book is a historical compendium of contributions to the Vineyard community by African Americans.

It was an exciting adventure to compile the accounts on these pages. As stories continue to emerge from the dusty archives of history, they breathe life into this document. It was a privilege to report my findings.

PROLOGUE

The experience of African Americans on Martha's Vineyard has proven to be a seemingly endless struggle, a saga of events not that different from episodes in other parts of the country, but unique because of the Island setting and the resort community that evolved on the Vineyard.

The early history of African Americans—enslaved by colonists to work the land, care for the house and rear their children—was typical of many northern states prior to the American Revolution. Life for African Americans across the country changed a great deal in the nineteenth century, with the Civil War and three key amendments to the Constitution. Yet segregation and subtle forms of racism persisted well into the twentieth century and beyond. And today, the issue of class distinction is a more relevant concern. For the African American population, the Vineyard was as challenging a place to live as anywhere.

As a unique resort community that attracted upper-class African Americans, the Vineyard began to define its own environment, typified by two leaders who arrived on the Island about 1900. Since then, vacationers have visited the Vineyard, first from Boston, then from New York and now from all over. The Vineyard truly has evolved into a haven for anyone seeking respite from the crush of humanity and the crunch of reality.

In July 1989, *Ebony* featured a spread on Martha's Vineyard and asked, "What is it about this island that makes it a magnet for Black vacationers? According to Islanders, what Martha's Vineyard has, what Black folk flock to the island to absorb, and what they hope to take home is a little piece of their history, their glamour and their roots."

Jackie Hammond concluded her piece in the *Intelligencer* on African Americans, "Bless all those hardworking, fun-loving souls who preceded us and thus made possible our days in the sun on Martha's Vineyard." That's what this book is all about.

ACKNOWLEDGEMENTS

Whenever an author sits down to write, he becomes beholden to a host of associates, friends and unknown contacts who lend their advice and knowledge to his endeavor. They earn no financial reward, but achieve recognition by offering their contribution to the cause and perhaps feel a token of generosity for furthering a literary endeavor they endorse. Otherwise, they wouldn't help out.

A number of people offered their assistance:

Cynthia Meisner, librarian at the *Vineyard Gazette*, opened her file drawers with envelopes on myriad topics in my research. She was most generous with her time and assistance. And thanks to Eulalie Regan for assembling many of those envelopes.

The cast of the Martha's Vineyard Museum, from Dana Street to Linsey Lee to Susan Wilson, offered direction and focus in research of this project.

At the Oak Bluffs Library, former research director Mat Bose was more than willing to seek out that missing piece, which led to assemblage of the total puzzle.

The staff of the Vineyard Haven Library was very accommodating in my need to use the microfiche for ancient copies of the *Vineyard Gazette*, which proved much easier than scrambling through boxes of yellowed papers, as I did for *Mystery on the Vineyard*.

Mary Sicchio, of the Falmouth Historical Society, offered information on the antislavery movement, the background of Charles Bennett Ray and a pertinent piece on petitions.

Lee Blake, of the New Bedford Historical Society, steered me on board the Underground Railroad, even to the Vineyard, and traced the route of Frederick Douglass as he lectured across New England.

Paul Cyr of the New Bedford Public Library provided access to relevant census information.

Tom Wallace of Wallace & Co., Sotheby's International Realty graciously allowed publication of his photo of President Obama at the Gay Head Light.

Chris Baer, who authored *A Hole in the Bible*, permitted republication of his story, first printed in the *Dukes County Intelligencer* in Autumn 2009, a publication of the Martha's Vineyard Museum.

Conversations, in person, by phone or online, added depth to this document. I particularly want to acknowledge the input of Chris Baer, Thomas Bennett, Adelaide Cromwell, Fran Finnigan, George Gamble, Melissa Hackney, Robert Hayden, Ben Hubert, Bob Hughes, Diane Jones, Francine Kelly, Chris Murphy, Laurie Perry-Henry, R. Andrew Pierce, Betty and Keith Rawlins, Estella and Mickey Rowe, Vera Shorter, Woollcott Smith, Joyce Stiles-Tucker, Robert Tankard, Mabelle and Sam Thompson, Olive Tomlinson, Lee Van Allen, Buddy Vanderhoop and Bob Woodruff.

Photographic images were a challenge. I want to thank my wife, Joyce, Florin at Mosher Photo, Bob Aldrin and Martha at Tom Wallace & Co., Sotheby's International Realty.

Particular thanks go out to Jeff Saraceno and Hilary McCullough of The History Press for guiding me through this mission. And I anticipate another energized sales promotion working with Dani McGrath.

And finally, and fortunately, I had the benefit of a sensitive ear from my wife, Joyce, who graciously listened to my plaints, calmed my fears, nurtured my dreams and penciled her corrections. Without her, this document would still be an open file on the computer.

Chapter 1

CHATTEL

The sound of gunfire echoed off the variegated cliffs of Gay Head, on the southwest corner of the island of Martha's Vineyard. A young man was drawn to the sound of the shots and hurried from his home on the shores of Squibnocket, a great freshwater lake not far from the clay cliffs. Anxiously, he peered around the bushes that cluttered the tops of the cliffs, curious at the unfamiliar blasts of musket fire below.

He watched as Her Majesty's Ship *Cerberus*, a twenty-eight-gun frigate of the Royal Navy, chased an American sailing ship, which was laden with supplies. The English ship fired on the American coaster, and after a small skirmish, the coaster erupted in flames. Or perhaps the Americans set the ship afire to prevent capture. It was difficult to determine what was happening from his secreted vantage point, more than 150 feet above the shore. The young man witnessed the crew from the *Cerberus* board small barges and paddle after the coaster, intent on extinguishing the fire to seize the supplies, before the ship was fully engulfed in flames.

Given the height of the cliffs, covered with shrubs and small bushes, the young man, whose name was Sharper Michael, observed a neighbor, one Abner Mayhew, dash down the clay escarpment to the beach below and begin to shoot at the redcoats in their barges. Sharper felt a surge of loyalty to join Mayhew and protect their homeland from the invading British. And now the British returned fire at the rebellious colonists. From atop the cliffs, Sharper Michael seized a gun and opened fire on the British barges. His brave efforts, allied with Mayhew's gunfire, caused the British sailors to turn back and retreat to their mother ship. It was a proud moment for the young Vineyarder.

Sharper Michael stood on the cliffs of Gay Head and fired at the British redcoats. Two hundred years ago, the clay cliffs stood 150 feet above the shore. *Photo by Joyce Dresser.*

The captain of the *Cerberus* was outraged at the audacity of the Vineyarders and vowed to seek revenge because they had fired on Her Majesty's Ship. John Symons recorded in his log on September 1, 1777, that "Our boats went and burnt the vessel," which, the captain claimed, was loaded with rum, sugar and other war supplies.[2]

***

Sharper Michael was born a slave in the town of Chilmark on Martha's Vineyard in 1742, the son of Rosa, an African slave owned by Zacheus Mayhew. Sharper's father most likely was Caesar Michael, from Guinea (b. 1709), another slave owned by Mayhew. Zacheus Mayhew intended to set Sharper Michael free, and with that understanding, Sharper moved from Chilmark to Gay Head, now Aquinnah, where he was living at the time of the skirmish. The Bristol County Supreme Judicial Court noted, in 1816, "Mayhew agreed to emancipate him, but no Bond was given…as required by the statute regulating the emancipation of slaves."[3] Sharper fathered two children with another slave, Rebecca, owned by Cornelius Bassett of Chilmark. Their children were Nancy and James Michael.

Zacheus Mayhew, Sharper's master, was only one of many Vineyard slaveholders in the 1700s. He was involved in the town militia and elected captain. Sharper's father, Caesar, served in the militia in the late 1750s, under Zacheus, who was listed in town records of the 1730s as a licensed innkeeper in Chilmark. Zacheus's brother, Zachariah, also served as a captain in the militia, but spent his time primarily as a missionary to the local Native American Wampanoags.

Sharper got around. After he moved to Gay Head, he married Lucy Peters, a Native American, in November 1775; they had a daughter, Marcy, born the next year. They may have also had a son, Cesar.

As a freed slave, Sharper Michael was accepted by the community of Gay Head, and his act to repel the invasion by the crew of the *Ceberus* was certainly a heroic deed, recognized and greatly appreciated by his neighbors. Unfortunately, Sharper never lived to earn credit for his bravery. He died from "a wound which he received in his head by a musketball," according to a witness of the attack.

Years before, the King of England had commissioned maps to be drawn by captains of British ships patrolling along the coast.[4] The accuracy of those early maps was amazing. At the time of the skirmish with the *Ceberus*, the cliffs rose higher and protruded farther out to sea than they do now. The clay cliffs sag with groundwater but do not erode as quickly as the nearby sandy shores. When Sharper was standing on the cliffs, the ground may have been squishy but still firm to the foot. And because of these early maps, Captain Symons of the *Ceberus* knew the coastline and was prepared to meet and intercept the American cargo vessel.

Sharper Michael's efforts went unrecorded at the time. A newspaper story in the *Vineyard Gazette* reported the attack, decades later: "In the meantime, a negro procured a howitzer with which he began to bombard the invaders from the cliff above and they were finally compelled to draw off without having effected their purpose…with so many wounded that they must tow one of the barges out." Sharper was credited with repulsing the invading British.

The article continues: "The Englishman [ship] was highly incensed at being thus paid back in his own coin and stood off and on all day, shelling the coast, but the only damage he [the British ship] did was to a negro whose curiosity led him to the cliff to see what might be doing and got in the way of an English ball."

Sharper Michael proved his heroism, even as he was "cut down in his prime, the first Vineyard casualty in the colony's struggle for independence."[5] It is of

17

note that this may have been the only casualty of the American Revolution on Vineyard soil, as the other recorded invasion occurred the following year, in the autumn of 1778, when General Grey sailed his armada of British warships into Vineyard Haven harbor and demanded local farmers turn over their sheep and cattle. Some ten thousand sheep were marched down Island to the harbor and led aboard ships, which sailed off to Newport, Rhode Island, where the sheep were killed to feed the British in the winter of 1778. No casualties occurred on the Vineyard in that incident.

Sharper Michael was the first Vineyarder killed in the American Revolution, and, like Crispus Attucks, who was shot and killed by the British in the Boston Massacre of 1770, he was an African American. And, as an African American defending his homeland from attacking forces, Sharper Michael exemplified the conflict of a slave, or former slave, who rose to exhibit brave deeds in a crisis. Yet the story of his bravery bears the underlying tone that Sharper Michael was once a slave, right here on Martha's Vineyard.

***

The story of Sharper Michael's progeny is a winding tale with numerous detours and distractions, as it meanders through several generations of African Americans on Martha's Vineyard. Unfortunately, few records remain of African Americans who were enslaved, and their stories are limited to worn and weathered slips of paper that record a financial transaction between two white people over the ownership of a black person. The best we can do is to acknowledge these faded forms of servitude and wonder whom the people were who lived under the yoke of slavery.

The issue of slavery as an economic force is debated to this day. Economist Paul Krugman recalled a professor who argued there is no point in enslaving people if they have nothing to offer, but if there is cotton to plant, ground to till, labor to be done and a financial gain to be made, it is possible to make a profit off the variance between what the slaves produce and the cost of their upkeep. That is the economic rationale for slavery.

The earliest notice of a slave transaction[6] on Martha's Vineyard occurred on August 24, 1703, when Samuel Sarson, grandson of Massachusetts governor Thomas Mayhew, sold an African American woman, valued at twenty pounds. We have no idea of her name, age or what became of her.

Chattel

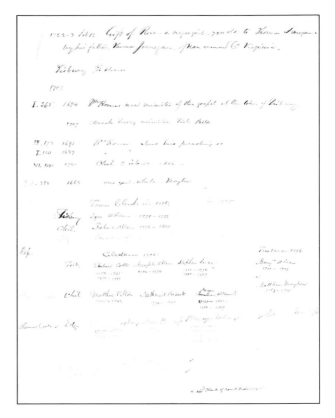

A familial transaction, dated February 12, 1722, reads: "one neager garll a Bout sevauen years old named Rose." This "gift" was presented to Thomas Jernegan by his father, Thomas Jernegan Sr. of Virginia. *Courtesy of the Martha's Vineyard Museum.*

The Martha's Vineyard Museum has a document that reads, "Know all men by these presents that Zach. Mayhew, Esq. for 150 lb gold paid by Ebenez Hatch of Falmouth, Bargained, Sold and Delivered unto him a negro boy called Peter, the said Negro Boy to have and to hold to the use of the said Eben Hatch's heirs, executors administrators and assigns for Ever." It was dated June 19, AD 1727, and signed by Zacheus Mayhew, the slave master of Sharper Michael. At the bottom of the page an addendum reads: "boy will be 11 years November 2, 1727."

Another listing revealed that Ebenezer Allen of Chilmark, who at one time held an innkeeper's license, owned negroes valued at £200. This was dated December 4, 1734. A will from Joseph Chase, also housed in the museum, details the specifics of his estate, including "one Negro boy." It was dated January 5, 1741. That same year, a Jane Cathcart of Chilmark granted freedom to Ishmael Lobb, apparently a slave on her land.

Across Vineyard Sound, a bill of sale in Falmouth, dated December 17, 1745, reads, "Then receivd of benjaman gifford forty shilings in Cash of

"An account of my estate, so follows one House, one Barn and Land of 10 acres and… one Negro Boy." This was listed in Joseph Chaces's estate. *Courtesy of the Martha's Vineyard Museum.*

ye old tener towards freeing my negor boy fortunatious sharper by name, att the age of thirty five years as witness my hand. John Hammond."[7] The archaic spelling does nothing to diminish the horrors of servitude and the sale of human beings as personal property.

Another fragmented document, also from Falmouth, and undated, is a pitiful petition from an African American slave named Cofe the Negro, who pleads that he has "a very great desire to be free from my Bondag which I have lived so long in" and goes on to state that he "should be very thankfull if the people would be of such bountifull hand as to contribute something To me." More than thirty Falmouth residents donated small sums of money for Cofe's freedom.

The saga of slavery continued on the Vineyard, with the sale of Black Manoel to a pair of Yankee sea captains in August 1768. The transaction assured the captains that "I bought [Black Manoel] on the Island of St. Michaels without any element of sickness" and that the slave was sold for a quantity of whale oil "to said gentlemen for being fully satisfied of his value."

Charles Banks, in his mammoth *History of Martha's Vineyard* (1911), noted the slaveholder Abraham Chase, ferry operator, owned four negroes valued at £54. Colonel Cornelius Bassett, who also held an innkeeper's license, once owned a negro appraised at £300. He was the slave master who owned Rebecca, the African slave who bore two children with Sharper Michael.

Chattel

A statement in the Martha's Vineyard Museum files reveals that on October 10, 1778, one Marshal Jenkins "Rec'd of Beiah Norton 26 lb 11 shilings and 1 peney in full ballance for Zeb Crafman and my Negro Mingdlas." Even with eighteenth-century spelling and English currency, we understand that Mingdlas was sold as a slave.

Ms. Hammond made a telling observation as she recounted numerous financial transactions in the sale of slaves on the Vineyard. "As property," she wrote, "it seems, slaves were documented with even less care than most land holdings."

On occasion, mitigating circumstances acknowledged a hint of humanity in this barbarous system. An article described a house once owned by Isaac Daggett, located in Scrubby Neck, across from the present airport. "He was a slave owner, it is said and had a male slave named Caesar." Daggett was fearful he would lose his human property, so he "offered to grant Caesar his freedom for $15, which offer was accepted." Caesar settled nearby, and the area became known as Caesar's Field.

And then there's Rebecca, the African woman who bore two children with Sharper Michael. Intermarriage was common between African American slaves and the Native American population who flourished in Gay Head, Christiantown and Chappaquiddick Island. When black men or women intermarried with Native Americans, the African Americans obtained rights to tribal lands. And that is what happened to Rebecca.

Rebecca, or Beck as she was known, was taken from Guinea in West Africa, survived the grueling ordeal of the middle passage to America and became a slave on Martha's Vineyard. She was owned by Colonel Cornelius Bassett of Chilmark. The timeline of her life is sketchy, but at one time Rebecca was married to Elisha Amos, a Wampanoag also known as Jenoxett. Rebecca and Elisha had no known offspring. Elisha had substantial property holdings, including land around Roaring Brook, a farm in Gay Head and a home in Christiantown. When Elisha died, in 1763, he willed some property, his livestock and home to Rebecca, his "beloved wife," for the rest of her life. Thus, during her lifetime, she was a landowner and a slave simultaneously. The field nearby was known as Rebecca's Field. This site is now the Land Bank property of Great Rock Bight Preserve off North Road in Chilmark. A plaque in Rebecca's honor was placed along the pathway, reading, in part, "Rebecca, woman of Africa, She married Elisha Amos, a Wampanoag... [and] died a free woman in this place in 1801."

Yet Rebecca Amos was also a slave of Colonel Cornelius Bassett, who lived at what is now Flanders Farm, farther up North Road, also in

Rebecca inherited property from her husband, Elisha Amos, at what is now known as Great Rock Bight. Yet she was a slave for Colonel Bassett at this farm in Chilmark. *Photo by Joyce Dresser.*

Chilmark. And it was during the period between Elisha's death in 1763 and Sharper Michael's death in 1777 that Rebecca and Sharper spent time together. It is believed that Rebecca was the first person to spot General Grey's warships as he approached Holmes Hole in the autumn of 1778; she sounded the alarm.

When Colonel Bassett died, in 1779, Rebecca's children with Sharper Michael, Nancy, age seven, Pero, age eighteen, and perhaps a third child, Cato, were sold in a slave auction to Joseph Allen of Tisbury. Rebecca died in 1801, a free woman, and apparently owned that property for the duration of her life, living in the house and working the land. And that's where the Michael family saga pauses, temporarily.

***

At the beginning of the Revolution, about six thousand slaves lived in Massachusetts. Yet the population of African Americans on Martha's

Vineyard was very small. Most of the people who came to the Vineyard of their own volition were drawn by employment as mariners or laborers.

Charles Banks compiled population figures for the latter part of the eighteenth century. Because only three towns were incorporated at the time, the numbers are distorted when compared to current statistics. Edgartown included Oak Bluffs prior to 1880. According to Banks, the first census was conducted in 1765. The total population of Edgartown was 1,030, of which 20 were listed as negroes, 12 male and 8 female. The first United States census of 1790 counted a total of 1,356 residents in Edgartown, of whom 10 were listed as "other free persons," presumably African Americans.

In Tisbury, which included West Tisbury until 1892, of 838 people in the 1765 census, 9 were negroes; the 1790 census listed 7 out of 1,135 residents. For Chilmark, which included Gay Head, now Aquinnah, of 546 residents in 1765, 17 were negroes, and twenty-five years later, in 1790, only 10 of the total 770 were negro.

Clearly, the African American population on the Vineyard was miniscule in the late eighteenth century. Of the 2,414 residents counted as Islanders in 1765, only 46 were of African descent, or just under 2 percent. And in 1790, when the census recorded a total population of 3,261, only 27 were African American, well under 1 percent of the population. This drop could be attributed to underreporting, reclassifying African Americans as Native Americans or considering some African Americans still as property, although slavery was deemed illegal in Massachusetts following the Revolution.

***

Slavery was effectively abolished with the adoption of universal rights under the constitution of the Commonwealth of Massachusetts. The Massachusetts Constitution, approved in 1780, contained a bill of rights that declared, "All men are born free and equal, and have certain natural, essential, and unalienable rights." This sounds very much like the Declaration of Independence. The Massachusetts Constitution was actually written by one of the men who wrote the Declaration. It spells out "the right of enjoying and defending their lives and liberties; that of acquiring, possessing, and protecting property," and concludes with a resolution "of seeking and obtaining their safety and happiness." This document was authored by none other than John Adams and is the oldest constitution in continuous use in the world.

The constitution outlawed slavery in Massachusetts, although that was not the specific intent of the legislature, which adopted Adams's efforts. A number of legal challenges and judicial decisions interpreted the wording of the constitution, which led to the abolition of slavery in Massachusetts.

Three cases involved a slave named Quock Walker, who was promised freedom by his master, Caldwell, of Worcester County. But Caldwell died before he could manumit, or emancipate, Walker. Caldwell's widow remarried, and the new master, Jennison, denied Walker his freedom. Walker escaped, was captured, beaten and returned to servitude in 1781. Walker sued Jennison for assault and battery, arguing that he was a free man based on the Massachusetts Constitution. Jennison claimed that Walker was his property and requested a writ of replevin, meaning the return of unlawfully obtained property; furthermore, Jennison maintained that slavery was necessary to subdue a barbaric people.

Walker was represented by Levi Lincoln, Esq. (1749–1820),[8] who argued the case with more depth and emphasis than simply the question of a previous promise to grant Walker his freedom. Levi Lincoln argued that slavery itself was a violation of the laws of nature and of God.

Chief Justice William Cushing concurred with Lincoln's argument that the constitution granted citizens rights by which slavery could not exist. Cushing's notes included the phrase "there can be no such thing as perpetual servitude of a rational Creature."

The jury determined that Walker was "a Freedman and not the proper Negro slave" because Walker had been promised his freedom and Jennison should have known that. The argument stated that the constitution guaranteed equality and freedom for "all men."

The chief justice affirmed the decision of the jury, with an additional statement: "Without resorting to implication in constructing the constitution, slavery is…as effectively abolished as it can be by the granting of rights and privileges wholly incompatible and repugnant to its existence." No effort was made by the legislature to amend or revise the constitution. Public sentiment strongly opposed slavery. Thus, slavery was effectively judged unconstitutional in Massachusetts in 1783.

African Americans had managed to take one small step on the road from slavery to emancipation, at least in the Commonwealth of Massachusetts, by the end of the Revolution. For African American residents of Martha's Vineyard, the ruling assured their eventual emancipation. It laid the groundwork for future activity of the African American community, as well as the framework for establishment of the abolitionist movement, which was gradually gaining ground across the North.

Chapter 2

ABOLITION

The experience of John Saunders on Martha's Vineyard speaks to the vicissitudes of the conflicting roles African Americans have had to play, both on Martha's Vineyard and on the mainland stage. In brief, John Saunders came to the Vineyard from the South, made a positive contribution and then met an untimely demise.

His story deserves to be told. John Saunders, an African American, and his wife, Priscilla, who was half white, were slaves in Virginia who managed to purchase their freedom in the 1780s. They sought to leave the South and secured passage aboard a ship captained by Thomas Luce of Tisbury. Captain Luce later tragically lost his eyesight in taking a solar observation and was called "the blind man." Although the Saunderses were allegedly free African Americans, Captain Luce offered additional protection when he hid them in the ship's hold: he covered them with corn. The year was 1787.

When Captain Luce sailed into Holmes Hole, as Vineyard Haven was known at the time, John and Priscilla Saunders decided they would debark. They "repaired to a house of Colonel Davies in a schoolhouse nearby the campground," in the Eastville section of the Vineyard, overlooking Vineyard Haven harbor. The Saunderses had two children, a son and a daughter. They felt accepted by the Vineyard community of the late eighteenth century.

John was not a minister, but he ardently preached the word of God. "A devout Methodist, Saunders, a zealous speaker and exhorter, 'preached to the colored people at Farm Neck.' He and his wife were held in high esteem during the five years they lived there."[9] In short, John Saunders brought Methodism to the African Americans of Martha's Vineyard long

John Saunders stood on Pulpit Rock when he preached to the African Americans who gathered round. This was a treeless plain two hundred years ago, and the glacial erratic landmass likely stood higher on the ground. *Photo by Thomas Dresser.*

before it was promulgated among the white population of Wesleyan Grove in the 1830s.

It was important to preach not far from where your congregation resided, as transportation was a challenge in the late 1700s. According to Jackie Holland, "In 1787, a number of Negro families had established a community in the Farm Neck area, between Sunset Lake and Farm Pond." Pulpit Rock Road is off County Road in Oak Bluffs; that is where John Saunders preached.

Saunders stood on Pulpit Rock, a glacial erratic landmass that dominated surrounding fields, then barren of trees. He exhorted or urged his parishioners to follow the tenets of Methodism. Both John and Priscilla were "zealous Christians, Methodist speakers," according to Jeremiah Pease (1792–1857), a prominent Vineyarder of the nineteenth century, who recorded stories about early religious efforts on the Vineyard. The assemblage of African Americans on the surrounding grounds was duly impressed by Saunders's passion for the word of God, even though it was filled with admonishment and dire warnings. His following may have been small, but his feelings were fervent.

Priscilla Saunders passed away in 1792. She had worked closely with her husband to raise their children and establish a base of religion. Shortly after his wife's death, Saunders moved to Chappaquiddick Island, just off the eastern shore of Martha's Vineyard and part of Edgartown, where he settled into a community of African Americans and Native Americans and, it is assumed, continued to preach Methodism.

John Saunders married Jane Dimon (Diamond) on Chappaquiddick. She was a member of the Wampanoag tribe. They had a daughter. In a journal allegedly kept by Saunders's granddaughter, Priscilla Freeman claims, "All three children [one being her mother] were said to have been of good character and to have embraced Methodism." This journal is no longer extant, but the page that describes Saunders's demise was discovered in the files of Jeremiah Pease, whose own journal recorded memorable events of this era.

All was not well on Chappaquiddick. Shortly after Saunders settled in with his new wife, he was murdered by the local Native Americans. Apparently, they were enraged that he had moved into the tribal area and married one of their own. This was the outcome of events as reported in Priscilla Freeman's journal. The murder of this martyr, as Priscilla refers to her grandfather, occurred either in 1793 or 1795. Records of the event are hazy at best.[10]

***

John Saunders was not the only African American who struggled and suffered in the early days of emancipation in Massachusetts. Nancy Michael (1772–1856), daughter of Sharper Michael and Rebecca, lived a challenged life on the Vineyard. Her story surfaces frequently in court records, which document a life of poverty and social segregation in which she was ostracized time and again.

Nancy was born in 1772. As noted, seven years later she was sold as a slave to Joseph Allen of Tisbury when her master, Colonel Bassett, died; when she gained her freedom from Joseph Allen is unclear. Her brother, James Michael, was a mariner who earned enough money to purchase a house in Edgartown in 1795. It is believed that Nancy lived in her brother's house, perhaps when he was away at sea. She may have rented out rooms.

In the early 1800s, Nancy had two daughters by different men and married neither. Rebecca Ann was born in 1803; Lucy Ann in 1808. In the years of her daughters' births, "Nancy sued two different men for support of her two children who she stated had been conceived at her brother James' house in Edgartown. Her 1804 testimony called him [her brother] James Sharper, while her 1808 testimony called him James Michael." Nancy Michael named Charles Whellen as Rebecca's father and Henry Anderson as the father of Lucy.[11] Lucy's life fades from the annals of history, but Rebecca survived.

In 1812, records indicate that the town of Edgartown supported Nancy Michael, the girls' mother, as she was listed as a pauper. In a court case four decades later, Edgartown sued Tisbury for payment of support rendered, but Tisbury argued that Nancy had been born free, although Tisbury admitted that Joseph Allen "owned her," since he had purchased her as a slave in 1779. When James Michael, Nancy's brother, died, Nancy inherited his house but sold it in 1819, apparently to pay back the town for support.

Nancy's half sister, Marcy, was the daughter of Sharper Michael and Lucy Peters. Marcy had three children, one of whom was Harriet, born in 1801. In a court case in October 1816 in Bristol County, inhabitants of the town of Westport, located between New Bedford and Fall River, Massachusetts, sought damages from Chilmark for the support of Harriet Michael in 1813. Court records indicate that Harriet was "a poor person found…in Westport, standing in need of relief…having her legal settlement…in Chilmark."[12] The question before the court was which town was liable for payment. Harriet was the granddaughter of Sharper Michael; had he survived the skirmish at Squibnocket, would he, could he, have provided for his children and grandchildren?

Again, we pause in the tale of the Michaels to allow the rest of the Vineyard to catch up. While African Americans were deemed free from bondage in the state of Massachusetts, that did not ensure them freedom from want. And across the country, slavery was very much the law of the land. Nevertheless, abolitionist sentiment began to grow in the North, even on the Vineyard.

***

George Washington owned slaves. He complained that he suffered economic hardship whenever a slave escaped his plantation. Efforts were underway to assist African Americans to free themselves from the bonds of slavery and lead them north to safety, but the efforts were intermittent in the early 1800s. Massachusetts certainly set the tone for the fervor of abolitionists when it outlawed slavery, but for struggling, illiterate, southern African Americans, that was small consolation.

The seeds of abolition had been planted and gradually started to bear fruit. Paul Cuffe (also spelled Cuffee) (1759–1817) was an African American Quaker merchant and fervent abolitionist from Westport. Cuffe was one of ten or eleven children born free on Cuttyhunk, one of the Elizabeth Islands adjacent to Martha's Vineyard. His father, Cuffe Slocum, was an Ashanti of the Ghanian ethnic group in Africa, captured at the age of ten and owned as a slave by a Quaker, Ebenezer Slocum of Dartmouth. Paul Cuffe's mother was a Wampanoag woman, Ruth Moses, from Gay Head on the Vineyard.

Cuffe was a successful boat builder and whaling captain and lived a life filled with adventure. During the Revolutionary War, he was held prisoner by the British. In 1783, he married Alice Piquet, and they raised eight children in Westport. As a captain, his ship was seized by pirates. He transported slaves on his schooner *Alphia* from Norfolk, Virginia, and Savannah, Georgia, to northern ports. He is credited with much of the success of the Underground Railroad in southeastern Massachusetts. And he smuggled goods from Canada.

With his profits secured by his maritime exploits, Cuffe took stock of his fellow African Americans. Because he had to pay taxes on his profits, he argued that he had the right to vote. Eventually, he earned that right. He had not been well educated as a child and sought to do better for his children. In Westport, he built a school for local children, both black and white, perhaps the first integrated school in the country.

In his goal to improve the lot of his race, Paul Cuffe considered relocation of African Americans back to Africa, specifically Sierra Leone. In conjunction with members of the British African Institute, he sailed one of his ships to Africa. However, only a few dozen people made the trek, and the project was later scrapped.

During the War of 1812, Captain Cuffe disobeyed the embargo with Great Britain when he sailed through a blockade, and his ship was impounded by the Revenue Service. For this infraction, he was summoned to the White House to explain his actions to President James Madison. The captain claimed ignorance of the blockade, and the president accepted his apology. Madison actually was intrigued by Cuffe's plan to transport African Americans back to Africa.

While Paul Cuffe actively sought solutions to the situation of the free African American, many more people braved social mores and cultural challenges to free African Americans from the scourge of slavery. Across Vineyard Sound, in Falmouth, a group signed petitions to outlaw slavery. A report detailed boxes of petitions stored in the National Archives, signed by thousands of American men and women of the 1830s, to "protest the slave trade in the nation's capital, the admission of new slave territories like Texas, and the fact of slavery itself."[13] One Falmouth petition bore the signatures of seventy-three women, including one Anness Ray, an escaped slave. In the cause of human freedom, it read, "We have done what we could."

In Washington, southern congressional legislators tabled, ignored and opposed the petitions, not only because the legislators supported slavery but because the petitions had been signed by women. Southern legislators questioned a woman's right to petition, since she lacked the right to vote. All the petitions were tabled, without any opportunity for discussion. This gag rule was not rescinded until 1844.

John Quincy Adams, then an elected representative from Plymouth, Massachusetts, "defended the right to petition against slavery and the right of women to petition." It was noted that "not since women signed petitions advocating the boycott of tea before the Revolution had women been so political as in the 1830s."[14] Within the abolitionist movement, women realized they had the power to organize, gather in public and undertake petition drives, as well as speak out against their limited role in political society. "In working for the freedom of the slave, they became aware of their own lack of rights and the Woman's Movement was born."

And it wasn't just in Falmouth that people were organizing. An antislavery group flourished in the 1830s in Edgartown. The Martha's Vineyard Museum preserves records of the articles and constitution for an organization known as the Northern District Anti-Slavery Society. It is dated December 31, 1836. This faded document describes adamant feelings held by the petitioners in their efforts to abolish slavery nationwide. Repeating words used in the Declaration of Independence and the Massachusetts Constitution, the group stated: "We believe that God hath endowed all men an inalienable right to liberty and that this self evident truth which is set at nought by the practice of this nation has for many years been rapidly losing its hold on the public mind and there is danger that it may soon be buried beneath the corruption induced by slavery." It was a clear statement of purpose, designed to ignite the fire of abolitionist speakers and work for the freedom of African Americans across the United States.

The document defines the goal of the signers: "We, the free inhabitants of Edgartown, freely impelled not only by duty to the oppressed and the oppressor, but to ourselves and our children, do form ourselves into a society. The object of the society shall be the entire abolition of slavery throughout the United States and the elevation of our colored brethren in the country to their proper rank as men." Looking at slavery as an abhorrent insult to the American dream, these Edgartown idealists sought to guide the law of the land because they believed, fervently, "that slave holding is in all circumstances a sin against God."

The group flaunted the name of their organization, the Northern District Anti-Slavery Society in Edgartown, but the short list of signers indicates that the organization did not have broad community support. The list does include a few old Island names: John Beetle, Samuel Butler, Benjamin Davis Jr., Charles Kidder, Edward Linton, Joseph Linton, Benjamin Luce and Constant Norton. In 1837, the president of the group was Thomas Cooke.

One article in the society's constitution referred to the separation of the sexes, even as the group tried to free the black man. "The female directors shall have the exclusive supervision of those anti-slavery efforts which may be made by the female members of the society." And the society planned for the long haul, as the annual meeting was scheduled for the third Monday in November.

The Northern District Anti-Slavery Society submitted a petition to the Massachusetts House of Representatives to grant freedom to African Americans held as slaves. Members of the society filed into the legislative chamber at the State House, in Boston, where the petition was ceremoniously placed on the speaker's desk. Charles Francis Adams, son of President John Quincy Adams, was a member of the Massachusetts House; he worked diligently in the legislature for passage of a Personal Liberty Bill, but such legislation did not take place until 1858, on the cusp of the Civil War. Yet the Edgartown petition was another rung on the ladder to reach full citizenship for African Americans.

In a related document, the society petitioned the United States Congress to take action via interstate commerce. It was a unique way to deal with the economics of slavery: prevent slave trade and slavery will eventually die on its own from lack of new slaves. The petition to Congress read, "Pray your honorable body, so to exercise the Constitutional power vested in you, 'to regulate commerce among the several states,' as entirely to prohibit the Domestic Slave Trade." The petition failed to rouse or rile Congress, but did make a point.

The society sought to interject its opinion in the annexation of Texas as a state. Since the Missouri Compromise of 1820, when Maine was admitted as a free state and Missouri as a slave state, the United States Congress had been consumed by agreeing on a compromise on the issue of slavery. The Northern District Anti-Slavery Society petition was signed on December 21, but no year was listed. Texas became a state in 1845.

The Edgartown antislavery group was irate that its petition to prevent the extension of slavery in Texas would not be heard in the House of Representatives. As noted, that august body chose to ignore, bypass, overlook or make no decision on issues that related to the abolition of slavery. The anger of the antislavery group from Edgartown echoed sentiment voiced in Falmouth that their petitions had been ignored by legislators.

Another document, also housed in the Martha's Vineyard Museum, makes reference to an African American whose freedom was purchased by the citizenry of Boston. Dated February 1, 1843, the certificate is a "Mammouth petition on George Beatiner, who had been arrested as a fugitive slave and whose freedom had been purchased by citizens of Boston." The chasm between slave states and free states deepened, as individual cases of escaped slaves and freed African Americans put a face and a name on issues leading to war.

In the abolitionist newspaper the *Liberator* of August 4, 1837, Samuel Gould,[15] a Baptist minister of the American Anti-Slavery Society, filed a report on his activities on the lecture circuit: "I went by way of New Bedford to Martha's Vineyard, where I arrived Saturday evening, July 1st. Met with a hearty welcome." On Island, he felt he was treated with deference by everyone, "save one. He was no sailor, and not a gentleman, but a collector of customs at Holmes Hole, named Worth." Gould lectured at the Congregational church, and on the Fourth of July, "I showed that republicanism and patriotism demand the immediate abolition of American slavery. Examined the Texas affair. In the afternoon I discussed the safety and practicability of immediate emancipation." One can almost feel the zeal of his oration.

Gould presented several lectures on the Vineyard, speaking at Holmes Hole and twice in West Tisbury. Then, he wrote, "I crossed over to Falmouth, with Mr. Ray, an estimable colored citizen of Falmouth. Mr. Ray has navigated a boat on the Vineyard Sound for upwards of twenty years, and has the reputation of being the best navigator on the Sound. He has carried the mail between Martha's Vineyard and the main above twenty years." Ray was the wife of Anness Ray; their son was Charles Ray, a prominent abolitionist and African American newspaper editor.

Charles Bennett Ray[16] (1807–1886) was born in Falmouth and educated at Falmouth Academy. In the 1820s, he worked as an apprentice boot maker in Holmes Hole (now Vineyard Haven) under the auspices of Thomas Robinson in his shop at the corner of Union and Main Streets. Ray was often soundly whipped by shoemaker Robinson, but he learned the trade well and earned an income from it his whole life. In 1832, Ray left the Vineyard to enroll at Wesleyan University as its first African American student but was obliged to withdraw by white students in his first term.

Charles Ray became a Congregational minister and was active in the antislavery movement. Ray was described as "a small man of wiry frame, light of color, polished of demeanor, modest and effective as a public speaker." In the late 1830s, he served as editor of the *Colored American*. He wrote persuasive essays and editorials for his newspaper, which, at the time, was "the only paper in the United States devoted to the interest of the Negro published by a man of color." Ray was considered by a contemporary as a "terse and vigorous writer" as well as an "eloquent speaker, well informed upon all the subjects of the day."

"Yet prejudice against color," Ray editorialized, "prevalent as it is in the minds of one class of our community against another, is unnatural, though habitual." He looked out his window, watching two children play happily together, one colored, one white; that confirmed his belief that racism is not inborn. One of his arguments was that African Americans are citizens of the United States because they were born here; as citizens, they are entitled to reside here.

Mr. Ray was active in the New Bedford station of the Underground Railroad and worked tirelessly on behalf of the half-million free African Americans, urging them not to immigrate to Africa but to stay in the United States and build a life as citizens of this country. His efforts, both as a minister and a member of the Anti-Slavery society, were directed to assist the freedom and legal defense of African Americans. His daughter Charlotte exemplified her father's dream, becoming the first female African American attorney in the United States. For many years, Charles Ray was a minister in the Bethesda Congregational Church in New York and "lived until 1886, long enough to enjoy some of that liberty for which he so patiently toiled."

It was into this controversial environment that Frederick Douglass (1818–1895) emerged. An escaped slave from Maryland who made it to New York in 1838, Douglass soon found himself on the abolitionist lecture circuit, akin to the activities of Samuel Gould. Douglass became a leading spokesman in the movement. An itinerary for the first part of the year 1846 indicated that Douglass ranged across New England and used his sharp mind and persuasive voice to excite and involve as many people as possible in the antislavery movement, even sailing to England, where he enlisted enthusiastic supporters.

New Bedford was Douglass's base of operations, as it was a hotbed of abolitionism, a haven for slaves seeking safety in stations along the Underground Railroad. As slaveholding regulations tightened in the buildup to the Civil War, more African Americans made their way north, through New Bedford and on to salvation in Canada. Frederick Douglass spearheaded the abolitionist movement and was a dominating figure in abolitionist activities, as well as lending his influence to the nascent women's suffrage movement.

Douglass gained fame through the popularity of his autobiography, *Narrative of the Life of Frederick Douglass, an American Slave,* which he revised and reprinted several times during his long life, after its initial publication in 1845. And during the Civil War, he conferred with President Lincoln on the treatment of African American soldiers.

***

The Underground Railroad apparently conveyed a few passengers on the Vineyard, as well. According to an interview conducted by Linsey Lee with Captain Charles Vanderhoop Jr. in 2001, the captain recalled stories his grandmother told. "My great-great-grandfather William Adrian Vanderhoop was born in Suriname, Dutch Guiana. He was the first Vanderhoop to come here, and he married Beulah Ocooch Salisbury. He built the old Vanderhoop homestead—it was the post office and a store awhile back."[17]

Now his story gets more interesting. "Their house was a link on the Underground Railway. My great-great-grandmother, Beulah Vanderhoop, would help escaped slaves find their way free. She'd hide them in the barn— there was a false cellar underneath the barn floor." That took courage, because if Beulah were found out, she could face serious punishment.

Charlie Vanderhoop continued: "My grandmother told of who she worked with in Vineyard Haven—of course that's where the big sailing ships come in, Holmes Hole—and how they got them [escaped slaves] up here. Then they usually could get them out on the boats going back and forth to New Bedford carrying fish. I think it was a total of eight slaves that she saved."[18]

Further corroboration of this story was added in a conversation with Buddy Vanderhoop, who said that William, his great-great-great-grandfather, actually owned a ship that transported slaves from Africa, but after a few years William tired of the slave trade and moved to the Vineyard, where Beulah set to work freeing escaped slaves.

This puts the Vineyard in the thick of the action to assist slaves on the road to freedom. It certainly was a brave undertaking for a woman in Gay Head. And the tale continued. After the Civil War, when the slaves had all been freed, one of the women whom Beulah had aided returned to the Vineyard to express her appreciation to Beulah. Unfortunately, both Beulah and her husband William were quite ill, unable to care for their homestead. Captain

Abolition

Vanderhoop picks up the tale: "The woman went back to New Bedford and she came back with about eighteen people and they done all the haying and cleaning up of the barns and tending the garden. They stayed about two weeks and left everything in perfect order. So, although she done a great deal for them, they turned around and paid her back, and I think that's a wonderful thing that they done this." This is one of the more gratifying tales to emerge from the horrors of slavery.

***

A muddle of conflicting laws and mounting tensions faced Congress. It became increasingly difficult to appease both the slave owners of the South and the ardent abolitionists in the North. Once Texas was annexed in 1845 as a slave state, it was evident that an amicable agreement between the South and North was critical or war would be declared. Kentucky senator Henry Clay (1777–1852) was a key figure in moving the debate, along with Senators John C. Calhoun and Stephen Douglas. Clay engineered a treaty between North and South, known as the Compromise of 1850, which pleased neither side completely but did forestall the outbreak of war.

Key provisions of the compromise, enacted in September 1850, included the option of popular sovereignty, or local vote, to decide whether to allow or deny slavery in the New Mexico and Utah territories. In return, California would be admitted as a free state. Slave trade was forbidden in Washington, D.C., although slavery itself was permitted to remain in force.

One of the most critical aspects of the Compromise of 1850 was a significant expansion in and enforcement of the (second) Fugitive Slave Act, which required northerners to capture and return escaped slaves. This infuriated northerners who chose not to get involved, and so incensed, they joined forces with the abolitionist movement. The efforts by the Edgartown individuals of their Northern District Anti-Slavery Society succeeded in making a statement against slavery, which proved another tiny step on the long trek to abolition nationwide. And it was indicative of the growing sentiment that spread across the northern states. But there was a great deal more heartache and acrimony before emancipation of all African Americans.

Chapter 3
FUGITIVE

In the evening we bound her feet with a crowbar and tied her hands behind her, and put her down in the hold, and laid the hatches." So begins an interview with a crew member aboard the ship *Endeavor*, moored in Edgartown harbor in the summer of 1854. The woman in question was an African American, a slave who had escaped from one Thomas Wilkins of North Carolina. She made it as far as Boston before she was captured. Then, according to federal law at the time, she was put aboard the sloop *Endeavor* to be returned to North Carolina. Captain Nathan Bunn knew he was required to return runaway slaves, so he ordered his crew to tie up Esther and keep her below decks.

The story unfolded in the yellowed pages of the *Vineyard Gazette* of June 2, 1854. "How she got loose, we know not, but in the morning she was gone, with the sloop's long boat." To undertake her escape without assistance from the crew, or someone aware of her situation, would put Esther on a par with Harry Houdini, undoing hands and feet and stealthily making her way above deck and overboard to steal a small boat, row away and evaporate on an island where African Americans were few in number. The crew claimed they were all aboard, all asleep. One can only assume someone assisted Esther to gain her freedom and managed to loose her chains and abet her escape.

The *Gazette* spoke for the population of the Vineyard when it noted that "the public mind has been greatly occupied recently with several cases of reclamation of fugitive slaves." And there were several cases. What made fugitive slaves such a hot topic in the 1850s?

Fugitive

The federal government had been involved in the recapture of runaway slaves since the adoption of the United States Constitution in 1789. Slavery was the engine that drove the southern agrarian economy. It proved financially feasible, indeed lucrative, to the North, because the slave trade depended, primarily, on northern maritime investments.

The economic impact of slavery is spelled out deliberately in Article 4, Section 2, of the U.S. Constitution. The federal government mandated the return of slaves, though they were not named as such. A slave was "a person held to service or labour in one state,…escaping into another,… shall be delivered up on claim of the party to whom such service or labour may be due." In short, fugitive slaves were to be returned to their master, per order of the United States government. This statement was reinforced four years later with the (first) Fugitive Slave Act of 1793, which linked fugitive slaves with hardened criminals or fugitives from justice. Under the Fugitive Slave Act, a judge could determine the disposition of a runaway slave without a jury trial.

As noted, Massachusetts effectively abolished slavery in 1783. Abolitionists grew more outspoken in Massachusetts in the early part of the nineteenth century, growing in stature with the likes of Samuel Gould, Frederick Douglass and Paul Cuffe.

The tide was turning across the country, however slowly. In 1842, the Supreme Court ruled that only federal authorities had jurisdiction over cases that involved fugitive slaves. Massachusetts quickly passed a law that forbade state officials from involvement in the capture or return of runaway slaves. The commonwealth went so far as to deny the federal government the use of state prisons to house fugitive slaves.

While the Compromise of 1850 brought a modicum of reconciliation in the spread of slavery, it created a major disruption in handling fugitives. The reinforced and expanded Fugitive Slave Act, initiated by Senator James Mason of Virginia, established commissioners to coordinate authority in regional courts to enforce the law that fugitive slaves must be returned to their masters. Fugitives were denied the right to testify on their own behalf or permitted a trial by a jury of their peers.

A bounty of $10 was paid to reward anyone who turned a slave over to federal authorities. Based on the Consumer Price Index (CPI), that $10 bounty would be worth about $235 today, which made it appealing on an economic level. According to the law, any and all runaway slaves had to be returned to their masters. And who decided whether an African American was free? It was determined solely by the word of the slave master; slaves themselves had no rights in the matter. Any African American suspected of being a runaway was liable to face prosecution. The consequence was that any free African American, regardless of being a runaway, could be forced into reenslavement, which did occur.

If a federal marshal allowed a fugitive slave to run away or a citizen assisted in the escape of an African American by offering transport, housing or water, a fine of $1,000 could be levied. The local sheriff could raise a posse, under federal jurisdiction, to capture a runaway slave.

In the early 1850s, residents of Martha's Vineyard who defied the law of the land risked significant punishment if they offered assistance to an African American on his route to freedom. Any crew member of the *Endeavor* who provided aid to Esther in her escape from the ship's hold in the late spring of 1854 risked a $1,000 fine and six months in prison. Captain Bunn confirmed the words of his crew, which meant he either professed ignorance in their disingenuousness or a bound and shackled African American woman could make fast her escape, unbeknownst to a crew of hardened mariners.

The law furthermore exacerbated the role of white northerners because now, according to the new law, they were liable for prosecution if they harbored an African American. Thus, by simply abiding by federal law, northerners assisted in the continuation of slavery. This brought an increase in the abolitionist movement. Does one defy an unjust law or ignore human compassion? How can one reconcile the statement that all men are created equal with the fact that free African Americans can be enslaved again?

The case of Thomas Sims was ripe with conflict. Shortly after the penalties for disobeying the Fugitive Slave Act were strengthened, this twenty-three-year-old runaway slave was captured in Boston. Abolitionists were angered, but failed to act. Under police guard, in the early morning hours of April 12, 1851, Sims was led aboard the ship *Acorn* and returned to his master in Savannah, Georgia, where he was whipped thirty-nine times in the town square. This incident put a face on the runaway and embarrassed antislavery advocates. More than any other case, the Thomas Sims incident raised support in Boston for a more aggressive abolitionist campaign. By doing nothing, abolitionists saw the folly of their ways; the Sims case ignited them to a call for action.

The immediate outcome of the reinforced Fugitive Slave Law was that escaped African Americans made their way in great numbers to Canada rather than settle in the northern states. There was a decided increase in stations, or safe houses, along the routes of the Underground Railroad, which overall became more efficient and more secretive in abetting the escape of fugitive slaves.

Fugitive slaves now were only safe when they escaped to Canada. Many Canadians deplored the influx of slaves to Toronto. One estimate was that between eleven and twelve thousand slaves had settled in County Kent alone. "A large tract of land has been purchased for negro settlement," the *Gazette* reported, "portions of which are rented or sold to the negro." The article expounded on the local legislature, which sought to levy a poll tax on negroes, "as it does for all foreigners."

However, as the *Gazette* noted, the Canadian legislature will "discourage the promotion of any institution with the object and end whereof would be in junction with the abolitionists of the northern states, to bring about a severance of the American union." The legislature wanted to tax the escapees but opted not to pursue political involvement in the problems that plagued the United States. "As for giving up any slaves now in Canada," the article added, "or that may hereafter come into it, the thing is out of the question. It cannot be done... The slave hunter must be prepared for disappointment in this case."

By publicizing this statement from the Canadian legislature, *Gazette* editor Marchant legitimized the efforts of the Underground Railroad, which funneled escaped African Americans to safe haven in Canada. It was a brave stand and made clear that Canada was the desired destination in the travels and travails of many African Americans in the pre–Civil War era.

***

The Fugitive's Gibraltar is a comprehensive review of runaway slaves who reached the seaport of New Bedford. Author Kathryn Grover examined where they came from and the increase in the size of the African American community in New Bedford. Doubtless, the abolitionists gained a foothold with the expanded role of Quaker ideology. This led to further opposition to slavery, which may have been a sound theological decision. The city's seaport status made it appealing for a quick escape from a ship into the helping hands that led to freedom.

White abolitionists were drawn to the ideological challenge associated with slaves and securing their freedom. They differentiated between those African Americans already freed and those still bound by the tyranny of slavery.

African American abolitionists, on the other hand, considered slavery an issue of race, regardless of whether the person was a slave, a fugitive or a free man. In their view, free blacks were inseparable from slaves. "Abolitionists of color," wrote Grover, "at least in New Bedford, never separated themselves from the enslaved millions who lived in the South; from the first days of their organization as antislavery advocates, their declarations suggest their assumption that free blacks were inseparable in every respect from slaves."[19]

In the legislatures of several northern states, personal liberty laws were enacted to ensure that jury trials were provided to fugitive slaves and that they could utilize the right of habeas corpus, which is to question whether imprisonment is legal and binding. Judges could no longer accept the word of slave owners without question. Personal liberty laws also severely reprimanded statements of false testimony from slave owners. Massachusetts passed such laws in 1855

More dramatic events occurred across the Northeast. Riots involving fugitive slaves occurred in Boston, Syracuse and New York City.

There was great excitement in Boston. "The good people of Boston have been laboring under great excitement for a few days past, in consequence of the arrest of Anthony Burns, an alleged fugitive slave…Burns was arrested at the instance of his master, one Suttle, of Virginia. He is said to be an intelligent looking man of about thirty years of age." The local newspapers were filled with stories of the plights of fleeing African Americans.

Reverend Dr. Pennington, an African American minister, preached in New York City. Reverend Pennington received a letter from a Mr. Grove offering to sell his brother, "who was recently taken back to slavery from New York." The letter continued, "stating that he will await a reply before selling him to the slave drivers." Reverend Pennington, although a free man, had to decide whether to buy back his own brother or allow him to be returned to slavery.

In another instance, also in New York City, a federal marshal transported a fugitive by train into the city, but the slave apparently got away. "Bells were rung, and upwards of 2000 persons turned out and attacked the [railroad] cars. A negro was caught, but he proved to be a passenger, and so the matter ended." Hysteria reached new heights at the increased vigilance and prosecution of fugitive African Americans.

On the Vineyard, we learn of Randall Burton, another runaway slave on the move. The *Gazette* of September 22, 1854, carried the following story under the heading "A Runaway Slave." "The bark *Franklin* which arrived at Holmes Hole on the 12th from Jacksonville, Florida had a slave on board, who secreted himself in the hold, when the vessel was loading." Again, an African American fled under cover of darkness. "While the vessel was lying at anchor, he took a boat and made good his escape to the shore; since

This page from the *Vineyard Gazette*, dated 1854, contains reports submitted by other newspapers, akin to today's AP wire service. The story of Randall Burton was big news. *Courtesy of the Martha's Vineyard Museum.*

which his whereabouts have been known only to a select few." The unnamed African American was judged to be about thirty years old.

A week later the *Gazette* brought the story up to date: "The bark *Franklin*, was supposed to have a fugitive slave on board." Upon arrival at port in

Kennebec, Maine, "she was immediately boarded by a body of men who were prepared to take him and ensure his escape. When they arrived on board, they were told that the slave has escaped at Holmes Hole." Apparently no one was aware the slave had slipped ashore on the Vineyard. A report the following week phrased the escape with the words that the fugitive slave had "left the bark clandestinely at Holmes Hole, with the boat, and had not been heard from."

The *Worcester Spy* added detail to the story, which was reprinted in the *Gazette*. It said that "Capt. Cook made every effort to find a U.S. officer to whom he might commit the slave. He sent information to the Custom House, and waited several days in Holmes Hole for an opportunity to return the negro to bondage." Paperwork required by the Fugitive Slave Law made it a challenge to handle in a timely manner, which, in this case, aided the fugitive by allowing him time to get away.

Captain Cook added his report to the growing body of gossip and innuendo regarding the runaway slave concealed aboard his ship. The captain claimed a severe gale had forced him to take refuge in Holmes Hole harbor. Captain Cook had dutifully requested assistance from the deputy collector to "have the negro disposed of according to the laws of the United States."

The deputy collector, Henry Pease Worth (the same man Samuel Gould found contemptible), composed a letter to the U.S. commissioner. Captain Cook waited dutifully for the paperwork to be processed and returned from the commissioner. Meanwhile, "the negro, or others for him, contrived to make his escape, carrying our stern boat, and since which neither boat or negro have been heard from." It would seem that a paperwork delay hindered an effective capture of the fugitive.

The slave had been secreted aboard the vessel for the five-day trip from Florida. "He gave his name as Randall Burton, and claims to be 31 years of age; was born in Williamston, North Carolina[20] and had been living for twelve or fourteen years on the Mississippi," reported the *Gazette*. The slave escaped from his master the previous October and was hidden aboard ship by stevedores in Jacksonville, Florida.

The *Gazette* concluded its reportage: "He landed on West Chop and proceeded to Gay Head, where he entered a swamp and remained concealed for several days." An arrest warrant was issued, and Sheriff Lambert began to pursue the man for stealing the *Franklin*'s small boat.

The story gathered momentum. Two women "emerged from the lovely village of Holmes Hole." They assembled pertinent supplies, such as food, a woman's dress and a bonnet, and hitched a ride out to Gay Head. "They had heard of the slave, and were determined to save him from capture, if possible." The slave came out from the swamp, met the women and, after a bit of persuasion, donned the disguise of a woman's dress and bonnet and entrusted himself in their care. The three were driven in a cart out to Manainshe (Menemsha) Bite, where they boarded a boat, secured by the women, and set sail across Buzzard's Bay. Sheriff Lambert arrived too late.

"After the arrival of the boat at New Bedford, the women took the slave to the residence of an abolitionist," the *Gazette* added, "and arrangements were made by him, which resulted in the forwarding of the slave to Canada." It sounded like a clean getaway.

An off-Island newspaper weighed in with a description of the runaway, full of salient and gleeful comments, again reprinted in the *Gazette*. The *New Bedford Standard* reported, "We are very happy to say that the fugitive in question arrived safely in this city, and is now in a place of safety."

A letter to the editor of the *Gazette* two weeks later noted Sheriff Lambert was a just and fair officer. "We have no doubt of Mr. Lambert's firmness. He is well known as an efficient officer." That statement explored, again, the danger the runaway faced from a determined sheriff, and how the two women put their own lives in jeopardy to rescue the fugitive.

***

A third incident of an escaped slave took place across Vineyard Sound in Falmouth. The story was spelled out in an article based on an oral history taken by Amelia Lawrence.[21] It recounts the tale of Dinah and events that unfolded in the old Falmouth post office. This story was initially delivered at a meeting of the Falmouth Historical Society on September 7, 1910.

"On the September day [no year listed] that her master was preparing to take his family and possessions back to the South, he took Dinah with him to the post office to obtain a permit to return her from a free state to a slave state." The law required certain paperwork to permit a slave master to transport his slave, legally, across state lines.

"Falmouth women in the kitchen of the private home that housed the post office drew Dinah into the kitchen with them, told her she would be free if she stayed in Falmouth. Offering to hide the willing girl, they rushed her to the cellar and stationed her behind a big pork barrel. Quickly, they then pretended to help the searchers."

The captain of the slave owner's ship sent word he had raised the sails and was about to head out of Falmouth harbor. The tide had turned, and he could wait no longer. The slave owner dashed from the post office to his waiting ship and set sail.

"Renaming herself, Anness later married a young man of mixed blood who carried mail between Falmouth and Martha's Vineyard. They lived in a small house behind the post office, which was then on Palmer avenue."

This last part refers to Joseph Ray, who delivered mail in his small sailboat between Falmouth and the Vineyard. He was the same man who ferried abolitionist Samuel Gould across Vineyard Sound in 1837. And Anness was a signer of the Falmouth Anti-Slavery petition of 1839, which gives perspective to the timeline of this adventure. These were the parents of Charles Bennett Ray, the ardent abolitionist.

Chapter 4

EMANCIPATION

In 1852, the Town of Edgartown sued the Town of Tisbury in Dukes County Court over money spent to support Nancy Michael, listed in the *Vineyard Gazette* as "a colored pauper." Edgartown claimed that Nancy was a resident of Tisbury, so Edgartown was not liable for her support payments.

The case was summarized in the *Vineyard Gazette* of June 4, 1852: "A special jury appeared for the trial of this act, composed wholly of Chilmark men. The action was brought to recover a sum of money alleged to be due from the defendants for support furnished one Nancy Michael, a colored pauper." This referred back to the 1812 case, when Edgartown supported Nancy and her two young daughters.

The plaintiff, Edgartown, argued that Nancy was the daughter of Rebecca, a slave of Colonel Cornelius Bassett of Chilmark. "Said Rebecca's child fell into distress [i.e., poverty] in the town of Edgartown, in 1812, which town brought a suit for damage against the town of Tisbury and recovered." So Edgartown won the case yet never received payment. And records of the Barnstable Court, which housed the old case, were consumed by fire in the 1820s.

Tisbury, in defense, argued that Nancy was born free, citing case law "that persons born slaves before slavery was abolished in Massachusetts, were, after the abolition of slavery, held to have been born free." This ignored the fact that Nancy had indeed been used as a slave owned by Joseph Allen for a number of years prior to the abolition of slavery in Massachusetts.

The court ruled that "said Nancy was free at the time she was sold to Joseph Allen and acquired as resolution thereby." In rebuttal, the plaintiff, on behalf of Edgartown, stated that if Nancy were deemed free and the

Supreme Court of Massachusetts determined she was a resident of Tisbury, there was insufficient documentation to prove a settlement. The case was carried over to the Supreme Court, #6563, which met in October 1852.

Nancy's daughter Rebecca, born in 1803, just prior to when her mother was deemed indigent, had a son, a William Martin, born in 1827 or 1830 (records do not agree on the year). Rebecca's life was filled with incidents of alcohol abuse, public disturbances and debt, not dissimilar to her mother's encounters with the law. When Rebecca died in October 1854, however, Jeremiah Pease noted her death in his diary. She was "about fifty," according to Pease, and passed away in Eastville, Oak Bluffs. It was unusual for a minister to record the passing of an African American, so Rebecca must have been a neighbor or meant something to Jeremiah Pease. Pease was also the one who reported the martyrdom of John Saunders on Chappaquiddick.

With her financial life strewn across the courthouse steps and pages of the *Vineyard Gazette*, and her daughter now deceased, Nancy Michael had little to live for. Her own death occurred at the end of 1856.

"Mrs. Nancy Michael, known to most of our readers by the familiar cognomen [name] of 'Black Nance' is no more." The *Gazette* considered her "a very remarkable character in her day" and then qualified the comment with the words "by many of whom she was looked on as a witch." The explanation of her bewitching powers evokes superstitious expressions that many people still practice, such as knocking on wood for good luck.

"She professed to have the power of giving good or bad luck to those bound on long voyages," the obituary continued, "and it was no unusual thing for those about to leave on whaling voyages to resort to her, to propitiate her favor by presents, etc. before leaving home." In a seaport, this power of superstition, of wishing for good luck before venturing out to sea, was certainly not unusual. "Her strange power and influence over many, continued till the day of her death," the *Gazette* intoned, although she had been confined to her bed the past three years. Nancy Michael died at the age of eighty-four.

In summing up her life, the *Gazette* repeated its opening observation that "taking her all in all, she was a most singular character." The closing lines are akin to the final words of a sermon in her memory: "May her good deeds long live in our remembrance, and her evil be interred with her bones."

From a seven-year-old negro girl sold as a slave—"Nancy brought eight pounds" in auction—to her life as a woman "long familiarly known to the more elderly readers of the *Gazette* as Black Nance or Nancy Michael," her presence in the community was duly recognized. And at her death, "with her passed the last relic of slavery on Martha's Vineyard."

Emancipation

***

From the genealogical travails of the Michaels we now review how the United States evolved from a slaveholding economy to a society that granted freedom to all its citizens.

A key court case in the years just prior to the Civil War was the Dred Scott decision by the Supreme Court, handed down in 1857 by Chief Justice Roger B. Taney. Just as the Fugitive Slave Act of 1850 riled the North into increased antagonism toward slavery, the Dred Scott decision created even more tension between the South and the North with its denial of rights to African Americans.

The ruling stated, bluntly, that African Americans imported to the United States as slaves, and their descendants, were not protected by the Constitution of the United States and could never become citizens. And because African Americans were not citizens, they had no right to sue. Furthermore, as slaves they were considered personal private property, chattel, and they could not be removed from their masters without due process, through their masters. They were forbidden from escaping the perpetuity of slavery and denied the rights of citizenship.

And so it was that four short years later, in April 1861, war broke out between the North and the South. Slaves were now caught in the midst of the struggle to preserve the union. Southern masters were at war with the Federal government, leaving slaves on their own. In 1862, an act was passed that any slave of a master disloyal to the Federal government, i.e., a Confederate, was considered a free man. Yet the Fugitive Slave Act was still in force, so residents in the border states, especially, faced the challenge of whether to return or harbor a fugitive slave. In 1863, President Lincoln issued the Emancipation Proclamation, which effectively freed all African Americans from bondage. By 1864, the Fugitive Slave Law was repealed, so Northerners no longer faced punishment for abetting a slave's escape.

The Emancipation Proclamation was a key element in freeing the slaves. At the time, however, it was considered a controversial measure. Initially, it was designed to grant freedom to slaves in any state that did not rejoin the Union prior to January 1, 1863. It was designed to lure the states that had seceded back into the union. In that area, it failed. Another element of the proclamation provided freedom to slaves in ten specific states, the heart of the Confederacy. Again, this was controversial because the Union had no authority over such states; that's what the war was all about. States under Federal jurisdiction were not included in the proclamation, which made the document pointless for them. Nevertheless, the proclamation did release about twenty thousand slaves from bondage on its effective date of January 1, 1863. The remaining four million slaves were freed as Union forces marched deeper into the South, but it was a slow process that dragged on for two more years.

***

The Vineyard was not immune to the requirement to furnish soldiers to fill Union ranks. In mid-May 1863, the *Gazette* carried a notice that all men between the ages of eighteen and forty-five were required to enlist. As the war grew more intense, the need for men became more critical. Each town had to meet a recruitment quota. Some men paid a bounty for an off-Islander to fill their slot, but many Vineyarders accepted their duty and enlisted. The obelisk at Memorial Park in Edgartown is a tribute to the Vineyard soldiers who died in the Civil War.

Through the summer of 1862, "the policy was clear. It was a white-only army. But soon the reality of the battlefield forced Lincoln to take a fresh look. It was obvious that blacks, especially freed blacks from slave states, were a source of manpower that could no longer be ignored."[22] The bravery of the Massachusetts Fifty-fourth, the African American unit, in its effort to take Fort Wagner, which was intended to protect Charleston, South Carolina, in July 1863, was widely seen as a success story for African American troops.

Lincoln issued the Emancipation Proclamation. Effective January 1, 1863, the United States Army began to recruit and enlist freed African Americans. (The navy already recruited freed blacks to serve as orderlies.) The Confederate response was to announce that it would execute black prisoners and return former slaves to bondage.

In late summer 1863, Massachusetts governor John Andrew began to recruit a colored cavalry, the Fifth Cavalry. Early in 1864, the *Gazette* devoted much copy to the vicious murder of William Luce of Holmes Hole by Gus Smith but then reverted to news of the war effort. The need for more enlistments continued. On January 29, the *Gazette* reported, "We learn from a reliable source that a colored man from New Bedford has enlisted five men from Gay Head." The question arose: who gets credit for the enlistments, New Bedford or Gay Head? Another news item observed, "Two of the Tisbury substitutes have been rejected at Camp Readville."

Two Vineyarders, both presumed African Americans, enlisted with the Fifth Cavalry.

James Curtis, born in Westport, living in Edgartown, signed up on January 18, 1864. He served as a guard and orderly at regimental headquarters. James Diamond of Gay Head had been arrested for breaking and entering at Manter's store in Chilmark, sentenced to ten months in jail, escaped, was recaptured and pardoned on condition he enlist. The need for soldiers was that great.

The case of James Diamond was reported by the *Gazette*, in detail, under the headline "Pardoned": "James Diamond of Gay Head was pardoned on condition that he should enlist in the colored regiment at Readville." The reporter observed that his enlistment should be credited to Chilmark, being contiguous to Gay Head, "but probably Boston will claim him as she gobbles up all with compunity [without remorse]." Nevertheless, Chilmark received credit for Diamond's enlistment.

The Fifth Cavalry trained at Camp Meigs, in Readville, just south of Boston, where the Fifty-fourth had trained. Both Curtis and Diamond were forty-one years old, much older than the typical recruit of twenty-five. Training consisted of group maneuvers on horseback and the use of breechloading carbines, rather than the conventional muzzleloading rifle.

Being African Americans in the Union army was not easy. Besides the overt racism exhibited by a number of prejudiced officers, there was debasement built into the system. Pay was unequal, as whites received $13 per month, plus a clothing allowance, while African American soldiers were paid $10 per month, and their $3 clothing allowance was deducted from their pay. The $10 a month pay would be equivalent to $135 per month today, based on the CPI and inflation factors tarnished by the economic situation of the war.

The Fifth, which consisted of nearly one thousand men, trained as a cavalry unit, boarded the train from Readville in early May 1864 and headed for Camp Casey in Arlington, Virginia, to defend the perimeter of Washington, D.C. In City Point, Virginia, they provided security to a supply depot and protected a jail filled with Rebel prisoners but were then summarily demoted to an infantry unit, but not trained as such. They participated in a march to Petersburg in mid-June. Meanwhile, Private Curtis was hospitalized with consumption, akin to tuberculosis, and James Diamond suffered sunstroke, perhaps in the capture of a Confederate cannon. The Fifth moved on to Point Lookout, again guarding a prisoner of war camp.

Their exploits concluded months later, near the war's end in April 1865, when "the march into Richmond was a final moment of glory for the 5th Cavalry, at least according to its colonel."[23] Colonel Charles Francis Adams

Jr., grandson of President John Quincy Adams, considered it a successful conclusion to battle. The war ended within the week.

In April 1865, emotions on the Vineyard, as well as the country as a whole, rose to the heights of exultation and then quickly slid into the depths of immense sorrow. First, there was the Union victory in Richmond, the capital of the Confederacy, reported April 14, where bells were rung and flags raised. That was immediately followed by great sorrow at the assassination of President Abraham Lincoln, reported in the press on April 21. A $100,000 reward was offered for the arrest of John Wilkes Booth, who had not yet been captured, reported April 28. So much joy, and so much sadness, in such a short month. On the Vineyard, there was an advertisement for the eighth annual cattle show and fair scheduled for October 17 and 18, 1865. At least Vineyarders could look forward to the annual Agricultural Fair.

Private Curtis mustered out of the army on November 24, 1865, due to tuberculosis. He continued intermittent work as a mariner and died in 1876. Private Diamond was discharged on June 4, 1865, returned to the Vineyard to work in light landscaping the rest of his life and died in 1897.

***

Although the Emancipation Proclamation freed the slaves, it did not abolish slavery. The passage of the Thirteenth Amendment to the Constitution effectively outlawed slavery in the United States.

Locally, the *Vineyard Gazette* reported on the war with updates on battles and the advance of Union forces. Besides the war news, there was an aggressive movement to free the slaves through an amendment to the Constitution. On February 3, 1865, the *Gazette* reported, "The Anti-Slavery Amendment to the Constitution passed the House on Tuesday last." It had already passed the Senate, so now it was up to three-quarters of the states to ratify the amendment.

A week later, the *Gazette* wanted to celebrate that Massachusetts had voted in favor of the amendment, but notice was not received in a timely fashion, "owing to the lateness of the hour at which the mails are received in Edgartown." Notice did go out shortly, and a celebration took place at the passage of this amendment, which granted what the *Gazette* deemed "the removal of that which has been the main cause of this war." James Cooms Jr., editor at the time, promoted a celebration that acknowledged the abolition of slavery, that all men are free and equal, that universal human brotherhood was their goal and that Congress had passed the amendment.

By year's end, December 6, 1865, the Thirteenth Amendment had been ratified by three-quarters of the states—twenty-seven out of thirty-six—and the United States had legally abolished slavery.

Three years later, on July 9, 1868, the Fourteenth Amendment was ratified, which granted citizenship to African Americans and their descendants, thus repealing the Dred Scott decision. This amendment has been used in cases regarding due process, from parental and marriage rights to equal protection for all citizens. The Fourteenth Amendment provided the basis for the *Brown v. Board of Education* case (1954), whereby the Supreme Court effectively ended racial segregation throughout the United States.

Two years later, on February 3, 1870, the Fifteenth Amendment passed. It granted all citizens the right to vote, which cannot be denied on the basis of a citizen's "race, color, or previous condition of servitude." Use of the word servitude is as close as the amendment came to acknowledging slavery.

It was another half century before the second half of the African American adult population—females—achieved the right to vote. All women, black and white, were granted the right to vote in 1920, with passage of the Nineteenth Amendment.

***

Abolishing slavery, granting citizenship and allowing former slaves to vote did not create harmony for all African Americans. A case in point occurred at Wesleyan Grove Campground in Oak Bluffs in 1889. Martha James was refused admission to a cottage because she was of African descent. It was reported that "Martha James, colored," sought to rent a cottage, "being refused admission to the campground."[24] It was noted that a neighbor, Selectman Matthews, "quite naturally objected to having a colored lodging house next door to him." Was it a lodging house or simply a house where Martha James planned to lodge? In any case, another house was secured, outside the confines of the campground, "in which she is comfortably settled and more satisfied with that than the one in the campground."

The newspaper mentioned letters sent from an attorney to campground directors, on behalf of Ms. James, "reminding them as Republicans of their offence against the 15th amendment [presumably the Fourteenth is meant]."

This solemn group of African Americans stood by 45 Trinity Circle in Wesleyan Grove. It may have been a rented home or, more likely, a gathering following a service in the tabernacle by an African American preacher seeking funds for his church. *Courtesy of the Martha's Vineyard Museum.*

The article considered that "the whole affair has been unnecessarily exaggerated and the Campmeeting authorities misrepresented." Apparently the issue had been raised earlier, when a petition was circulated to deny leases to African Americans.

Previously, in 1887, directives of the Campmeeting Association were approved that stated, "we judge it improper and illegal to make distinctions among our tenants on the ground of color." The policy was clear, whether or not it was followed. It is in doubt whether Martha James indeed intended to open a boardinghouse. The article concluded with the "fact" that at least twenty-five lots were currently leased to colored people in the campground.

In late 1873, Methodist bishop Gilbert Haven, a white minister whose cottage still stands on Clinton Avenue in the campground, rode in a blacks-only train car through Mississippi to protest discrimination; this was something of a precursor to the Freedom Riders. He supported interracial marriage. President Grant resided in Haven's cottage when he visited the Vineyard in August 1874.

***

The nineteenth century was a period of tumult and upheaval for the country but a century of relief from the bondage of slavery and an opportunity for freedom for African Americans. Two Vineyard African Americans, a barber and a sea captain, worked diligently to assure their individual success and open doors for future generations of African Americans on the Vineyard.

William H. Hammond was a southerner who traveled from New Bedford to be married to Ellen Lang at Wesleyan Grove Campground in 1873. Within seven years, "Barber" Hammond, according to local historian and teacher Chris Baer,

> *began the haircutting business that is now Bert's Barber Shop. He built the building on the south corner of the plaza across from Zephrus on Main Street—the one now occupied by Sweet E's Cupcakes. He built it twice, actually, as the first building burnt down in the great fire of 1883, which destroyed nearly every store in Vineyard Haven. To the best of my research, "Barber" Hammond is the only African American business property owner in the history of Main Street, even to this day.*
>
> *Barbershops were relatively new to Vineyard Haven—until the 1870s barbering had been a more casual, part-time occupation. Hammond became a well-known and well-respected figure on Main Street. He was known as "the jolly village barber."*
>
> *Within days* [of the great fire of 1883], *Hammond had reopened his barber shop in a friend's shed, and within two weeks they had found the money from somewhere to purchase an additional lot to his north, next to the ashes of the old tailor shop…and reopened his doors to business. He lacked one necessary item, however—a barber pole—so he painted the red and white stripes on the street lantern out front.*
>
> *Then Ellen died, leaving Hammond alone and without family.*[25]

Barber Hammond took up with Marion Lair, wife of Captain Leroy Lair. The outcome of this liaison was that Marion Lair got pregnant and delivered an interracial baby, which must have caught her husband by surprise. "In the end, Cap'n Lair accepted him and chose to raise him as his son, and gave him not only his last name but also his middle name, Crosby." As Mr. Baer writes, "His [Lair's] lifelong dedication to Marion is well-remembered in our family, especially as she began a long slow descent into dementia in the final decades of life."

William Hammond remarried in 1906 but died in 1914, after a career of nearly forty years as a barber in Vineyard Haven.

Ralph Crosby Lair (1900–1965) was the son of Marion Lair and William Hammond. Ralph, who stood six feet two inches, proved to be an outstanding basketball player at Tisbury High and went on to play semiprofessional football as well as boxing and a bit of baseball. He was known as Lefty Lair. Yet Ralph waged a lifelong struggle with alcohol. He moved to New York and later Washington. He maintained intermittent correspondence with his half brother Stan, Chris Baer's grandfather, but died in Worcester in 1965. "My mother cried for a full day, mourning the uncle she never knew," writes Mr. Baer at the end of his memoir.

***

Phoebe Moseley Adams Ballou first came to the Vineyard in 1883 with her daughter Caroline. She managed to buy a house in Oak Bluffs, half a duplex, next to Call's Market (now Our Market) on the waterfront. The other half of the house was owned by the West family, parents of Dorothy. In 1909, a fire destroyed the house and caused both families to relocate, the Wests to the Highlands and Phoebe to Bellevue Heights, on Pacific Avenue. It was there that her granddaughter, the artist Lois Mailou Jones, summered, appreciating the spirit and beauty of the Vineyard many years later.

***

The whaling industry peaked in the mid-nineteenth century and then was gradually reduced toward the end of the century. It was decimated by the discovery of oil underground at Titusville, Pennsylvania, by whaling ships impounded by Union forces during the Civil War, by the invention of the electric light bulb and by the basic depletion of whales in the North Atlantic. But when it was in its glory, whaling was a most profitable enterprise to engage in.

"Black mariners found acceptance not based on their race, but as hard working and skilled seamen in an industry that was physically demanding, filthy, and often financially unrewarding at most levels,"[26] wrote Erich Luening on the challenges that faced nineteenth-century mariners. Only a very few African Americans attained the position of captain of a whaling ship. Three such captains are worthy of study.

Paul Cuffe, as we have seen, "set the bar for other African-Americans wishing to make their livelihoods on the high seas," according to Luening.

As a teenager, he labored on whaling ships, and after the Revolution, proved himself a prosperous merchant mariner.

Absalom Boston (1785–1855) was a whaling captain from Nantucket, the first to sail with a crew exclusively made up of African Americans. His most famous voyage was as captain of the *Industry* in 1822, when he returned from six months at sea with seventy barrels of whale oil.

William Shorey, born in Barbados in 1859, was known as the Black Ahab. As whales were depleted along the East Coast, whalers had to sail farther west, chasing the leviathans. Captain Shorey reached California and became the sole African American captain on the West Coast. He retired in 1908.

These three young whalemen—Jose Oliveiers, Antone Lopes and Antone Fortes—were hardy souls, hopeful for a profitable voyage. Mr. Fortes later worked as custodian at the Tisbury School. *Courtesy of the Martha's Vineyard Museum.*

Then there was William Martin, son of Rebecca Michael, grandson of Nancy Michael and great-grandson of Rebecca and Sharper Michael. Martin was the last of this family of African Americans who faced the challenges of slavery, poverty and racism yet rose to the heights of prominence and prosperity. Born in Edgartown, Martin attended local schools and developed a distinctive literary style, manifest in the copious logs he kept. Sailors recall "his quick, alert movements, and crisp, decisive speech, qualities which went far to make him a successful whaleman."[27]

One of the logbooks he maintained during has final voyage as captain of the *Eunice H. Adams* contains the following entry:

> *Saturday June 22* [1889]: *Begins with a calm. At 3 pm sperm whales were raised about 3 miles ahead of the vessel. Lowered the two port boats*

Captain William Martin's house is in a sad state of disrepair. A couple bought the house and the quarter-acre lot in 2006; their intent was to repair the structure and have it listed on the National Register of Historic Places. Instead, the house has been sold. *Photo by Thomas Dresser.*

and pulled to the windward, but could not head them off. The larboard boat got in ahead of one and tried to go on but the whale went down. Then the waist-boat went on to another and struck and was fast about five minutes when the iron drawed. Got the whale alongside at 9 pm. Later part very rainy and windy. Commenced cutting at day light. Sperm all round the vessel but the weather was too bad to lower. Finished cutting in at 9 o'clock. So ends this day.[28]

In 1857, William Martin married a Wampanoag woman, Sarah Brown. They lived with her family on Chappaquiddick Island, deigning not to build in downtown Edgartown, where more prosperous whaling captains erected elegant mansions along North Water Street. The Martins had no children, so the line from the slave Rebecca to Nancy and another Rebecca and now William Martin ended without issue.

Sarah Brown's great-great-great-niece, Penny Gamble-Williams, described the challenges her ancestors faced. The link between African Americans and Native Americans is evident in her story. "Chappaquiddick men were whalers historically. Whaling was one of the toughest jobs during that time and because the men were out to sea for long periods of time, sometimes years, it took a toll on the elders, women and children."[29] Her husband, Thunder Williams, added that with Native Americans at sea, others filled their role on land, intermarrying and becoming part of the tribal community.

Penny Gamble-Williams continued: "My great-great-great aunt, Sarah Brown, who was Chappaquiddick, married a black whaling captain, William A. Martin. His great-grandmother had been enslaved on Martha's Vineyard

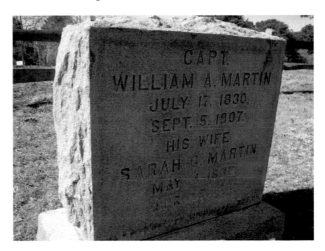

This stone faced away from the sea for years, perhaps as an insult to Captain Martin because of his skin color. Today the stone faces the sea, like the other graves in the cemetery. *Photo by Thomas Dresser.*

Island and was owned by the Bassett family." She went on to describe the Martins' house: "William and Sarah lived in a humble home that he built on Chappaquiddick. The house still stands and is privately owned. It needs major repair. There is no plaque showing the history of this black whaling captain."

Captain and Mrs. William Martin celebrated their fiftieth wedding anniversary on July 2, 1907. The *Gazette* duly reported the occasion, although in hushed tones, as Captain Martin was in failing health. They were recognized as "well-known residents of Chappaquiddick. Captain has been a paralytic for the past seven years and is now practically helpless. No celebration was planned."

Of his seafaring career, it was noted that Captain Martin was "known in shipping circles as a very skillful and capable whaleman." He sailed aboard the *Almira* and the *Europa* and served as first officer of *Clarice*. He was master of the whaling schooner *Emma Jane*, and his last journey was as captain of the brig *Eunice H. Adams*. Captain Martin died on September 5, 1907. His obituary was brief but poignant: "The services were largely attended, by practically all of that island and many from this village. Captain Martin, in his day, was a whaleman of very enviable reputation, and had sailed as master of several ships of Edgartown."

With the tale of William Martin, we conclude the story of four generations of African American Vineyarders who left their mark on those around them. Their lives were a tangled, twisted journey, but the route from the baseness of human servitude through the depths of poverty and lawlessness, to the height of prominence as captain of a whaling ship, is a rags-to-riches tale worthy of the efforts expended by these brave souls so many years ago.

Chapter 5
PACESETTERS

As Martha's Vineyard entered the twentieth century, two African Americans arrived in Oak Bluffs. Each made a lasting impression on the town. It is unknown if they were friends, competitors, allies or antagonists, but it is certain they knew of each other. And we know the outcome of their efforts had a major impact on the tiny African American community, which numbered fewer than 150 inhabitants in 1900.

Oscar Denniston was a preacher from Jamaica who reached the Vineyard in 1900 and served as pastor of Bradley Memorial Church on Masonic Avenue in Oak Bluffs for forty years.

Charles Shearer, a former slave from Virginia, bought land in the Highlands of Oak Bluffs about 1900, opened a laundry and then a guesthouse and catered to visiting and vacationing African Americans.

Each man made his mark. Their individual influence and impact was felt not only in the African American community but also across the Island.

REVEREND OSCAR DENNISTON (1875–1942)

Just as John Saunders arrived on the Vineyard at the end of the eighteenth century and spread the word of Methodism, so too Oscar Denniston came to the Island at the end of the nineteenth century to preach the tenets of the Baptists.

Reverend Denniston was born in Kingston, Jamaica. In the late 1890s, a Vineyard Haven chaplain, Madison Edwards of the Seamen's Bethel, was on vacation in Jamaica when he fell ill. Oscar Denniston, a seaport chaplain himself, cared for him. When he regained his health, Reverend Edwards encouraged Reverend Denniston to move to the Vineyard.

Oscar and his wife, Charlotte, arrived on the Vineyard in September 1900. He took a job as assistant[30] to Susan Class Bradley, a prohibitionist who had founded the Oakland Mission in 1890. She designed her mission to assist in the assimilation of the expanding population from Portugal and the Azores that had settled on the Vineyard. Upon Mrs. Bradley's death, in 1907, Oscar Denniston assumed leadership of the church and renamed it the Bradley Mission in Susan Bradley's honor. Oscar's son Dean recalled that his father was a true evangelist

One chaplain, Madison Edwards of Vineyard Haven, meets another. Reverend Edwards encouraged Reverend Oscar Denniston of Jamaica to move to Martha's Vineyard. He did, and the rest is history. *Courtesy of the Martha's Vineyard Museum and Doris Clark.*

and, as the new minister of the church, served all his parishioners, white, Portuguese or of African American descent.

"The chapel was on Masonic Avenue,"[31] recalled Dean Denniston. "We would have church meetings in the chapel attached to the house we lived in." Dean's sisters, Olive and Amy, played the organ; the parishioners sat on benches, which the Dennistons referred to as pews. Bradley Memorial Baptist Church was the first church specifically devoted to the African American community on the Vineyard, a group which made up about 4 percent of the year-round Vineyard population of four thousand people in 1905.

The great gramophone sits in stately silence behind the attentive children, patiently posing for their Sunday school photograph at the Bradley Mission. *Courtesy of the Martha's Vineyard Museum and Doris Clark.*

The Oscar Denniston family. *Left to right*: Madison, Reverend Oscar Denniston, Olive, Amy, Medora, Dean and Osmund, who drowned tragically in 1939. *Courtesy of the Martha's Vineyard Museum and Doris Clark.*

Oscar and Charlotte Denniston had three sons, but she passed away in 1905. Oscar returned to Jamaica. During his visit, he witnessed an earthquake and filed a piece that ran in the *Vineyard Gazette* in 1907: "The earthquake itself was horrible, dreadful, awful, but to think of the fire that followed immediately, was more awful." The quake occurred on January 14, 1907. Oscar returned to the Vineyard with a new wife, Medora Curtain, and they had five more children: Olive, Baron, Dean, Amy and Gerald.

Word of the popularity of the church spread across the Island. Dean recalled how a bus driver, George Bernard, on a Sunday evening, would drive a sightseeing bus all over the Island, from Oak Bluffs to Gay Head, West Chop, Vineyard Haven and Edgartown "to pick people up and bring them to church, making $5 for the shift." Vanderhoops and Diamonds came from Gay Head for the Baptist service.

As Dean Denniston recalled, "There were a lot of people of color that came to Martha's Vineyard to work during the summertime, and Sunday evening service was the big event." Service began at 7:30 and ran until 9:15 p.m. Dean observed that "to go to church was a sort of an activity. It was a reward for the end of one week and the beginning of the next." He appreciated that his father's service ended just after 9:00 p.m. so he could sprint up to Ocean Park and catch the final numbers of the weekly summer band concert.

The popularity of church services was well known, according to the *Gazette*, with parishioners gathering on the street outside the church and blocking traffic. "The small chapel in the house at Masonic Avenue became too small to fit the large group of summer worshippers, and so Oscar Denniston moved

The Bradley congregation gathered outside the church for a formal photograph. Many children participated in the service. *Courtesy of the Martha's Vineyard Museum and Doris Clark.*

summer services into Noepe Hall, which was erected in the late 1800s as a vaudeville theatre and dance hall." Reverend Denniston converted this old movie theatre into his church for summer services. That building was torn down in 1958. In the meantime, Bradley Memorial Church had converted the old Odd Fellows Hall, which, ironically, had formerly served as the first Baptist church in Oak Bluffs. In a sense, Reverend Denniston brought his church full circle, back to where the denomination originally flourished, on Masonic Avenue.

CHARLES SHEARER (1854–1934)

The life of Charles Shearer was epic. Charles Shearer was born a slave in Appomattox County, Virginia. His mother was an African American; his father was her master. As a ten-year-old in the midst of the Civil War, Charles was chained to a barn by his master/father and abandoned as Union troops approached. Freed by the soldiers, young Charles ingratiated himself with the soldiers by his knowledge of local hunting and fishing and showed them where to scavenge for food. From this auspicious beginning, Charles Shearer impressed the world around him.

Charles attended Hampton Normal and Agricultural Institute in Virginia, graduating and then teaching at the college. He met and married Henrietta Merchant, born free, who was part African American, part Blackfoot Native American and part white. The young couple settled in the Lynchburg, Virginia area, and both taught in nearby schools. In a letter to a friend at Hampton Institute in 1888, Henrietta referred to the need for books and clothes for her forty-five scholars. Over the years, both Charles and Henrietta maintained a close relationship with their alma mater. In an 1898 letter to Hampton, Charles recalled "the old school and its pleasant surroundings." Charles and Henrietta had two daughters, Lily and Sadie, and a son, Charles Jr.

In the 1890s, the Shearers moved north, buying a house in Everett, a suburb of Boston. "Through hard and honest toiling, I've been able to accumulate not less than $3,000," Charles noted. "I am heading my way upward." They joined the Tremont Temple Baptist Church, the first integrated church in the country. It was founded in 1839 with a policy not to charge for pews, a policy which made it possible for poor people to attend church. Tremont Temple Baptist defined itself as "a church with free seats where everyone, rich or poor, black or white, should be on the same religious level." Charles wrote that "according to duty [I] attend services when convenient."

Charles Shearer worked in the hospitality field, serving as maitre d' at Young's Hotel, owned by J. Reed Whipple, a Civil War veteran who had worked as a grocer in Roxbury. Shearer also worked in the culinary field at the Parker House, a Boston landmark since 1855. Both experiences proved key to future endeavors on the Vineyard.

About 1900, Charles and Henrietta visited Oak Bluffs because they had heard of the Baptist services at the tabernacle. They soon purchased property in the Highlands, near the Baptist Temple, which had been erected in 1877.[32] The Shearers' first house was a small bungalow and shed, which served as their summer vacation retreat on the Vineyard.

To help with expenses, Henrietta opened a laundry adjacent to their property that specialized in ironing the fancy fluting or French pleating of petticoats popular in the day. The laundry catered to wealthy white women who lived in the Highlands and proved so successful that Henrietta had to hire a staff of six local women. "The women who ironed at the Shearer laundry brought their own irons and kept their own stoves fired up."[33] Henrietta even orchestrated a delivery system with horse and buggy to make sure the linens were returned in a timely manner.

Henrietta Shearer used this carriage to deliver clean laundry in the Highlands; once Shearer Cottage opened, she transported guests back and forth from the ferry. *Courtesy of the Martha's Vineyard Museum and Lee Van Allen.*

Adam Clayton Powell Jr. stands on the left; also in this 1931 photo are Lillian Evanti, Hazel Thomas and Martha Robbins in the center. Charles Shearer is third from the right, near the dog. *Courtesy of the Martha's Vineyard Museum and Lee Van Allen.*

Yet the Shearers had a grander scheme in mind. In 1912, they built and opened a twelve-room inn, which they operated in conjunction with the laundry. Based on the hospitality experience Charles Shearer had garnered in the culinary arts of Boston hotels and Henrietta's laundering of linens, this was a sound investment. And it proved quite successful, since prominent African Americans who visited the Vineyard were denied rooms at the local hotels and inns because of their color. Shearer Cottage became the primary inn for African American visitors to the Vineyard.

And it was not just an inn. Shearer Cottage served family-style meals and offered airy rooms with white tieback curtains, a tennis court and an expansive front porch. Room and board was eighteen dollars per week during World War I. It became a haven for African Americans to stay and an opportunity for locals to work.

Daughter Lily married Lincoln Pope, and they had three children, Charles, Doris and Liz White. Charles died young, Doris proved a mainstay in continuing the operation of the cottage and Elizabeth White remained close to the family business, even as she promoted a summer theatre program

Harry T. Burleigh holds his hat; Charles Shearer is second from left, with daughters Sadie and Lily, second and third, respectively, from the right. This photo was taken in 1918, the year after Henrietta died. *Courtesy of the Martha's Vineyard Museum and Lee Van Allen.*

in the 1940s. Lily passed away in 1920, and her sister Sadie and Charles, the father, continued operations.

Henrietta passed away in 1917, and with her death, the family discontinued the laundry service. Doris Pope Jackson, born in Everett in 1915, recalled her grandfather, Charles Shearer. "I knew him well. Tall and straight and handsome. We spent a lot of time with him. He was articulate—you'd always see him in a starched shirt and tie and a Panama hat, always very proud. He was about six feet two. He was like a prince and he looked like one."[34]

By this time, 1920, Shearer Cottage was very well known in the African American community, both on and off Island. On Island, African Americans made up about five hundred individuals, or 10 percent of the population. Oak Bluffs itself was home to over one hundred African Americans, based on the 1915 state census. "The opening of Shearer Cottage gave a strength and endurance to the summer community of this period, as had the leadership of Reverend Denniston to the year-round residents."[35]

"The guests were very prosperous people,"[36] recalled Doris Pope Jackson. "And all of these blacks were very, very well educated blacks. Artists, judges, lawyers, principals of schools, teachers, congressmen; they all stayed up at Shearer Cottage." She was suitably impressed by

Above: The couple seated on the ground are Henry and Martha Robbins, frequent guests at Shearer Cottage. He was the court photographer in the Sacco-Vanzetti trial in 1921. *Courtesy of the Martha's Vineyard Museum and Lee Van Allen.*

Left: Guests enjoy the Highlands fresh air at Shearer Cottage. Martha Robbins is the woman in the middle. *Courtesy of the Martha's Vineyard Museum and Lee Van Allen.*

the clientele. "Everyone would dress up for dinner. Most of them were New Yorkers and they always dressed. That was fascinating to watch. Beautifully dressed and well educated."

***

James Henry Hubert (1886–1970) was the ultimate community organizer. The son of a Georgia slave, he graduated from Morehouse College in Atlanta in 1910 and attained a master's degree from Columbia in 1914. At that time, he was recruited by the Society for the Propagation of the Gospel Among the Indians of the Massachusetts Baptist Missionary Society and the Massachusetts Board of Education. He was asked to teach basic education to the Wampanoag Native Americans and preach as the lay pastor of the local Baptist church. Mr. Hubert was happy to teach but skeptical of the preaching. In any case, according to Dr. Lester Russell,

> *James Hubert went to work at Gay Head, Massachusetts in 1914. Shortly after he arrived on the island, he organized the Indians into a community organization, the Gay Head Improvement Association, and impressed upon them the value of education and religion to their lives. Within one year after he began work at Gay Head, practically every Indian house had a child in school. Every home had a garden and the entire community began to thrive and grow. In addition, James preached two sermons a week at the Gay Head Baptist church and brought many Indians into the Church.* [37]

Further research indicates that this statement exaggerates the impact Mr. Hubert had on the Gay Head community. The Native Americans already had a school, a church and a garden by every house.

Mr. Hubert taught and preached from 1914 to 1917 and bought property on Lighthouse Road in Gay Head, now Aquinnah. He left Martha's Vineyard for New York City, where he worked for the National Urban League. In search of funds for housing for impoverished African Americans who migrated from the South, he successfully approached John D. Rockefeller. Mr. Hubert's program evolved into the New York Urban League, and he served as its executive director from 1919 to 1943. His son Ben still enjoys the family home in Aquinnah.

***

The First World War was over. The Roaring Twenties had begun. Women now had the right to vote. And African Americans were making progress toward becoming accepted as a community on Martha's Vineyard, in great part through the impressive performance of Reverend Denniston. Word was out that the Island welcomed African Americans, at least at Shearer Cottage.

After thirty years of service, the religious leaders on Island, all Caucasian ministers, recognized Reverend Denniston for his service to the community. They gathered on a podium to commend his efforts. As reported by the *Gazette*, "The scene of sincere tribute to a Negro pastor of a Negro church was singularly impressive." Son Dean recalled that the congregation did include white people on occasion as well as Portuguese but was primarily comprised of African Americans.

But it was not a perfect place. Dean recalled that his father was named to fill an unexpired term of a seat on the local school committee when one of the members passed away. Oscar ran in an election, but as Dean remembered, "My father was defeated. He was defeated because he was a black man." Gossip fired the fear that were Reverend Denniston elected to the school committee, it would usher in black teachers to the schools. On recalling that memory, Dean noted that during the course of his lifetime, Martha's Vineyard has hired two superintendents of school who were African Americans.

A telling observation of Reverend Denniston was the tribute of his commitment to his congregation. "In winter and summer, in fair weather and foul, he walked the streets, calling on his parishioners and doing whatever he could to make life brighter for them." Oscar Denniston did his best to assist and inspire the African American community. After forty years of productive ministry, the *Gazette* noted proudly, "he has identified himself with his church and with the Vineyard, and he deserves well of all who love the Island."

For nearly a decade, Reverend Denniston found himself in failing health, and after a brief illness, he died at the age of sixty-six in the early spring of 1942. The *Gazette* opined that, "the side of his life that he kept chiefly to himself would have revealed many sacrifices for the good of others." But those sacrifices were rewarded many times over by the drive and determination of his progeny.

Reverend Denniston was a dominant religious leader in the community for four decades. In his obituary, which appeared in the *Gazette* on March 6, 1942, Henry Beetle Hough, editor, made the following observation in tribute to Denniston's dedicated career: "Out of his energy and taking up church work has developed a religious organization that has become an impressive Island institution." Reverend Denniston was a dedicated, dynamic individual. The *Gazette* continued, "His standing among the Island clergy, regardless of faith, was enviable; everyone admired and trusted Mr. Denniston." And he was "always keenly aware to civic duties and activities which might affect the public as a whole."

A final tribute to the life of Oscar Denniston concluded his obituary: "The career of Reverence Oscar E. Denniston…has left a bright mark in our community. His contributions—in sincerity of purpose, faith and staunchness through the years…Islanders should be proud that he lived and worked here." And, it was noted, "During his funeral service, all business in Oak Bluffs will be suspended."

Medora Denniston died in 1971 at age ninety-six. "She is remembered on the Island, especially in Oak Bluffs, for her active participation in the affairs of her husband's pastorate which he held for many years. During those years, Mrs. Denniston stood at his right hand in all efforts made in behalf of the church." Behind every prominent man stands a strong woman; Medora was a positive influence on her husband's career.

"One of the most impressive fruits of Mr. Denniston's career is the record of his children, almost all of whom had outstanding school and college careers," noted the *Gazette*. He certainly imbued his progeny with a strong dedication to further their education. Dean recalled, "All of us—my brothers and sisters—left Oak Bluffs to further our education. At one time there were four of us going to Boston University at the same time."[38] African Americans were denied access in the dormitories, so they found rented rooms. Education was that important.

Madison, a son from Oscar's first marriage, studied at Northeastern and Suffolk Law and worked at the YMCA in Boston. He and his wife, Lillian, "were summer residents of Martha's Vineyard since 1945." Olive Denniston, eldest child of Oscar's second marriage, taught at Barber Scotia College in Concord, North Carolina. Amy Denniston was a trainer at Florida Normal College in St. Augustine. Gerald Denniston, youngest child of Oscar, was a quality control analyst with the Social Security Administration. "He never failed to mention the beauty of the Island in any conversation."

Dean Denniston (1914–2006) was most like his father. He recalled the prejudice he faced in the course of his long lifetime. As a student, "never once did I get a chance or was I asked to participate in those school plays. The kids of color never had a chance to be in any of those productions. Never. Unthought of. It was just understood." Dean graduated from Oak

Bluffs High School in 1931. He was the "first African American to join white graduates on the high school's senior class trip to Washington, D.C., though he was not allowed in their hotel, rode in the back of the bus, and had to use segregated rest rooms."[39]

In a 1996 interview with the Martha's Vineyard Museum's Linsey Lee, Dean Denniston recognized reality. "You did find prejudice on Martha's Vineyard," he said. "It definitely was there. The Vineyard was second-hand prejudice. Unwritten. They didn't not allow you, they just were 'full.' They didn't have any room. 'All reservations taken.' That's back door prejudice." He recalled that blacks who worked in grocery stores worked in the back room and were not allowed to deal with the public. "You were behind the scenes. You did not wait on customers."

"I came out of high school right at the height of the Depression," Dean went on. "Those were some bad years." He remembered clearing brush in the state forest, earning fifty cents an hour, working for the Works Progress Administration. Then he went on to Boston University, where he earned BA and MA degrees. Unable to obtain a teaching job because he was African American, Dean worked as a dining car porter for the New Haven Railroad, Boston to Washington line. Over the years on the train, he met the likes of Dr. Martin Luther King Jr., John F. Kennedy, Marilyn Monroe, the Red Sox team (including Ted Williams), Jackie Robinson, Joe DiMaggio and Richard Nixon.

Dean's wife, Robbie, was a graduate of Tuskegee Institute and helped found the Cottagers, a philanthropic social organization in Oak Bluffs. Dean and Robbie had two sons and a daughter.

After his days on the New Haven Railroad were over, Dean worked as a special assistant in human services. He loved the Vineyard and often returned to the Island. "He greeted the Clintons during their vacation on the Vineyard and sat next to the President during the service."

Dean lived in Boston for seventy years and had tickets to the Boston Symphony for forty years. He died in 2006 at the age of ninety-two; his obituary in the *Gazette* contained the following line: "Mr. Denniston remained a lifelong Vineyarder, who became an unofficial ambassador for the Island by greeting people as they came off the ferries in Oak Bluffs and Vineyard Haven."

The Massachusetts Baptists kept Bradley Mission operating until April 1966. The current status of the Mission is that it has been purchased by the Island Affordable Housing Fund to "restore the building, creating a multi-use cultural space" with affordable residential units. The Island chapter of the NAACP is working with Affordable Housing on the mortgage to protect the building for future generations.

***

Shearer Cottage was *the* place to stay on the Island. If you were an African American visiting the Vineyard, Shearer Cottage was on your itinerary. "There's no place like it. Blacks like to be together, especially to have fun and relax."[40] The guest book reads like a who's who of the African American community. The likes of Harry T. Burleigh, A.C. Powell, Paul and Eslanda Robeson, Ethel Waters and Lillian Evanti, who sang opera as coloratura soprano, stayed there, along with eminent Boston attorney William Lewis, New York realtor J.E. Nail, Washington banker Doyle Mitchell and, of course, Reverend Adam Clayton Powell Sr., who first brought his son, Adam Clayton Powell Jr., as a boy of twelve in 1921.

As Doris Pope Jackson recalled her childhood, "And we, as teenagers, always worked up there. We waited on tables and cleaned the rooms. We did everything. We were trained to work when we were kids. And we enjoyed it. We were paid

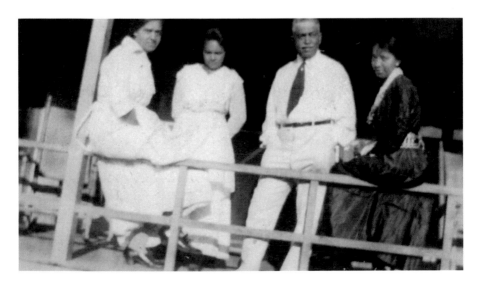

Harry T. Burleigh (1866–1949) cuts a commanding pose in this 1918 photograph on the porch of Shearer Cottage. Burleigh was a professional singer, a baritone, who introduced African American folk music to Anton Dvorak, who then incorporated it in his *New World Symphony. Courtesy of the Martha's Vineyard Museum and Lee Van Allen.*

The dining room staff at Shearer Cottage, about 1950. *Back row, left to right*: Louise Rice (Sadie Shearer's daughter), Olive "Cutie" Bowles, Olive Bowles Jr., unknown; *front row*: Edward Rice (Louise's son), Al Shearer. *Courtesy of Olive Bowles Tomlinson.*

A comfortable collection of Shearer guests, featuring Henry and Martha Robbins in the middle. *Courtesy of the Martha's Vineyard Museum and Lee Van Allen.*

for our work and loved to spend our money downtown in Oak Bluffs."[41] She went on: "There was always plenty of food. We laughed and talked and had a wonderful time. I was proud that my grandfather owned an inn."

As their website (shearercottage.com) notes, "On any given day, the dining room was filled with fifty or more guests, all enjoying delicious breakfasts and dinners cooked by Aunt Sadie [Shearer Ashburn], Uncle Robby [Merchant] and Uncle Benny [Ashburn]." In a *Gazette* piece, Olive Bowles, a member of the wait staff, was quoted, "We served 50 guests in one sitting at breakfast."

Olive Tomlinson, daughter of Olive and William Bowles, recalled a typical breakfast at Shearer Cottage: "Homemade New England baked beans, codfish cakes and Sadie's homemade rolls. All homemade. We would request extra desserts and then hide them in the closets to eat later." Sadie had two elderly men who "helped" out, but Sadie did all the work. The men would slide open a window that looked out on the dining room to check up on the waitresses. They were, according to Olive, "not the most pleasant looking of men." They were Sadie's second husband, Ben Ashburn, and her cousin, "Uncle Robbie."

Ms. Tomlinson remembers that prior to the big Sunday dinner, Sadie would pile all the kids in a car, an open car, and head out to the turkey farm. Sadie selected the turkeys and then brought them back to pluck, cook and serve. She also offered her guests homemade peach ice cream for dessert. Olive recalls that she wasn't as proficient a waitress as her mother, who could serve up to sixty people by herself; Olive shared the task with her cohort, Gail Jackson.

Lee Van Allen, who now runs Shearer, noted that "nearby, black-owned homes were often called upon to supply rooms for Shearer's overflow of guests. Indeed, many of the black homeowners on the Island have said that their presence here today is due to their earlier association with Shearer Cottage."

Shearer Cottage closed in 1971 but reopened in 1983. Now it is operated by Doris Pope Jackson, granddaughter of Charles and Henrietta, and Lee Jackson Van Allen, great-granddaughter. Shearer Cottage was the first site dedicated on the African American Heritage Trail, on September 2, 1997.

Charles Shearer and Oscar Denniston each made a positive impact on the African American community on Martha's Vineyard in the first third of the twentieth century. To have a place to stay was imperative to attract vacationing African Americans; to have a place to worship was integral to the heart and soul of the African American community. Both Mr. Shearer and Reverend Denniston were important people in spreading the positive word about Martha's Vineyard by making the environment on the Island hospitable to year-round residents as well as summer visitors.

Chapter 6

PROMISE AND PREJUDICE

Professor Adelaide Cromwell studied the evolution of the African American community in the seaside community of Oak Bluffs. She noted that the first African American residents lived on the Vineyard year-round and ensured that they had a church, which bonded the community.[42] That occurred through the efforts of Reverend Denniston. Even though fewer than five hundred African Americans lived in Dukes County, which comprises all of Martha's Vineyard as well as the tiny town of Gosnold on the island of Cuttyhunk, African Americans made up 10 percent of the total population in 1915.

A second contingent of African Americans came to the Island and worked for wealthy white people in the summer. These domestics flocked to the Bradley Memorial Church on Sunday evenings as well but did not intermingle with the year-round African Americans. They worked diligently through the summer. "Some year-round blacks worked for the wealthy white summer people, opening and closing cottages, as well as cooking, cleaning and taking care of their children." Ms. Holland graciously recognized the domestics. "Bless all those hardworking, fun-loving souls who preceded us and thus made possible our days in the sun on Martha's Vineyard."[43]

In 1940, a social group called the Open Door Club was formed for the benefit of the hired help. Edna and James South believed that African Americans who worked hard all week needed an oasis to get together socially outside of work. The group was started by domestic employees "to provide a means of social contact which was otherwise lacking and to make possible pleasant use of leisure time on Thursday and Sunday afternoon and evenings."

At its height, over sixty members participated in the afternoon gatherings, when the hired help had a half day off. The Open Door Club sponsored an annual picnic where black servants would invite their white employers, making it an integrated event, perhaps the first on the Island. At one Open Door meeting, a Mr. Hamilton was quoted as saying, "Sometimes I wonder if you who live here have consideration for the help who contribute to the enjoyment of your summer."[44] Hired help had neither money nor means to get to Oak Bluffs for a swim on their time off.

A third wave of African Americans, more wealthy than their predecessors, vacationed on the Vineyard beginning in the mid-1940s and were part of a leisure middle and upper class. They stayed as guests at black-owned lodging houses, primarily Shearer Cottage, and later bought their own homes. Ms. Cromwell first summered on the Vineyard in 1943 and still maintains a residence on the Island.

The summer people, like vacationing folk everywhere, descended and departed the Vineyard according to the schedules of the schools "back home." Initially, there was little social interaction between the year-round black population and the summer homeowners. Each kept to himself. Yet the relationship between the year-round and summer African Americans was decidedly warmer than with the domestics of the second wave. Ms. Cromwell observed, "Gradually, with the merging of the summer and year round black community under the spiritual and perhaps social leadership of Reverend Denniston, additional affluent black summer people began coming from Boston and surrounding areas."

Adelaide Cromwell was a friend of writer Dorothy West. Ms. Cromwell, in fact, wrote the introduction to *The Living is Easy*, Dorothy West's first novel. In the late 1920s, Dorothy West lived and wrote in New York City during the Harlem Renaissance, a unique era that occurred when an influx of African American intellectuals converged in New York City following World War I and remained through the Great Depression. The Harlem Renaissance was characterized by an impressive output of creative expression in art, music and literature and led to a broader awareness of the special talents of many African Americans, including Dorothy West.

On the Vineyard, Dorothy West was the first to write about blacks in a white newspaper without labeling the residents as colored. "To her they were just people doing things."[45] She described the wave of African Americans who vacationed on the Vineyard: "There were no separate areas. There were too few black vacationers to form a colony."[46] She recalled, "We were among the first blacks to vacation on Martha's Vineyard. It is not unlikely

This happy gathering of local children celebrated a birthday party at the home of Dorothy West in the late 1940s. Olive Bowles Tomlinson is on the swing, partially obscured. *Courtesy of Olive Bowles Tomlinson.*

that the Island, in particular Oak Bluffs, had a larger number of vacationing Blacks than any other section of the country. There were probably twelve cottage owners." Her pointed observations about the black Bostonians who frequented the Vineyard, of whom she was one, advised: "They were taught very young to take the white man in stride or drown in their own despair. Their survival was proved by their presence on the Island in pursuit of the same goal of happiness."

So the African American Bostonians had the Vineyard to themselves, with a few notable exceptions. Adam Clayton Powell Jr. of New York stayed at Shearer Cottage. Ms. Cromwell noted, "Even Powell led a relatively restricted life here, apparently enjoying the pleasures of fishing and the company of close friends more than the flamboyant role for which he was known in New York and later in Washington."

An influential visitor like Judge Watson, the first black judge elected in New York City, may well have talked up the Vineyard. As Dorothy West remarked, "Like all who have come to the Island in the years of their innocence, something here has touched them with sweetness and simplicity."

Most assuredly, Harry T. Burleigh enticed fellow African Americans to visit the Vineyard. "Harry T. Burleigh, the composer, left a priceless legacy in his long research of Negro spirituals," wrote Dorothy West. "He was the first to bring back glad tidings of the blacks' fair land to his New York friends, who had always thought of Massachusetts as a nice place to come from, but not to go to unless bound and gagged."

Barbara Townes, a lifelong Islander, recalled Mr. Burleigh's generosity. "Now we used to go downtown as children. Harry Burleigh—he was my godfather and he was a composer of spirituals. He used to come down here and stay the summer. He used to give us the money, give us two dollars for all the kids to go down to the movie."[47]

Word was out, and now African Americans from New York flocked to the Vineyard. Again, Dorothy West was ready, pen in hand, to describe the influx and the reaction of the staid, reserved Bostonians.

And then came the black New Yorkers. They had heard of a fair land where equality was a working phrase. They joyously tested it. They behaved like New Yorkers because they were not Bostonians. There is nobody like a Bostonian except a man who is one.

The New Yorkers did not talk in low voices. They talked in happy voices. They carried baskets of food to the beach to make the day last. They carried liquor of the best brands. They grouped together in an ever increasing circle because what was the sense of sitting apart. Their woman wore diamonds, when the few Bostonians who owned any had left theirs at home. They wore paint and powder when in Boston only a sporting woman bedecked her face in such bold attire. Their dresses were cut low. They wore high heels on sandy roads.

Dorothy West had no trouble expressing her opinion.

Olive Tomlinson was a New Yorker who first came to the Vineyard with her parents as a child in the early 1940s. And she remembers Dorothy West quite well. Olive recalled:

My mother was dear friends with Dorothy. She was my parents' age. All lived in the Highlands. All adults were Aunt and Uncle. We called her

Aunt Dorothy. She wrote many short stories. My mother managed her traveling outfit for talks and helped her with her speeches. Late in her life she would make outrageous social and political statements, but because she talked so fast, no one could understand—or believe—what she was saying. They had no idea what she was talking about.

"By the mid-1950s," Adelaide Cromwell noted, "Oak Bluffs was a heterogeneous black resort with summer visitors coming from all over the country and abroad." It added prominence that Senator Edward Brooke first came as a tourist in the 1940s, bought a house in Oak Bluffs in the 1950s and ran successfully for statewide office in the 1960s, prior to his election as the first African American senator since Reconstruction.

For some African American entrepreneurs, business proved profitable at the beginning of the twentieth century. John Pollard, a veteran of the Civil War, operated a dining room in the Highlands, catering to an upper-class white clientele. Besides Shearer Cottage, the landladies of Circuit Avenue, sisters Louisa Izett and Georgia O'Brien, ran boardinghouses for African Americans denied lodging in other hostelries. George Frye ran a profitable cobbler shop on Circuit Avenue for many years; the vacant site adjacent to Ben and Bill's Ice Cream was his place of business. Ambler Wormley operated a gas station and repair shop on New York Avenue from 1928 to 1946; it is now DeBettencourts. Wormley was born in Fredericksburg, Virginia, and lived more than fifty years in Oak Bluffs, once serving as commander of the local American Legion. "Mr. Wormley was well known and respected in his home town."[48] The few businesses owned by African Americans made a positive impact on the economy of Oak Bluffs.

***

Olive Tomlinson has written many memorable passages, both personal and public. As a child in Oak Bluffs, she fondly recalls her summers in the late 1940s and 1950s.

We headed first to the Corner Drugstore, with the long inviting soda fountain counter to ogle at Jack Welti, the cute counter boy…The fact that we didn't have money for the fountain fare didn't stop us from sitting at the counter, short legs dangling, and embarrassing him. We were also in awe

These young teens rode their bikes all the way out to Gay Head in 1953. The photo was taken by the late Preston Silva. *Left to right*: Adrienna McClane, Clo Guinier (Lani Guinier's half sister), Julie Simon, Gail Jackson (Doris Jackson's daughter) and Olive Bowles Tomlinson. *Courtesy of Olive Bowles Tomlinson.*

of the two beautiful counter girls; one was Grace Frye whose father owned the cobbler shop on Circuit Avenue. Then time for my secret prayer: please let me be a beautiful teen-age counter girl someday. [49]

From the Corner Drugstore, the youngsters visited the penny arcade, Darlings for popcorn and down to the beach at Church's pier. It was an idyllic way to spend a day.

One memory Olive holds from childhood was the embarrassment she felt when members of the Shearer Summer Theater staged a two-girl show for Olive and Gail Jackson, billed as Cookie and Candy, the Sweet Sisters. "Before an audience of friends and family Gail sang a cappella and I whirled like a teeny dervish." Olive adds, "I don't know how the adults contained their laughter."

For the adults, "Fives to Sevens" were cocktail parties held by African Americans, to which it was an honor to be invited but then an obligation to host. As many as one hundred guests would attend these gatherings, invitation only, and it was requisite that one dress up and do one's hair for a chance to see and be seen. The younger crowd was less intrigued by these events. "I never did Fives to Sevens," says Olive. "Same old same old. Our age group was much more interested in sports and activities and enjoying the Island. Much more active. Tennis. Bicycles. We did some parties at night." And Olive did enjoy the theatre.

***

A news item in the *Gazette* at the end of World War II, August 24, 1945, described a new Island theatrical event: "Negro Experimental Group to Present *The Women*." The article announced that the Shearer Summer Theatre Negro Experimental Group planned to present Clare Booth Luce's *The Women* at the Oak Bluffs school gym. "The play is staged by Elizabeth White, assisted by Doris Jackson, with Dorothy West as stage manager... Mrs. Sadie Shearer Ashburn is the advisor." That announcement was the inauspicious opening for a theatrical ensemble that lasted fifteen years and provided decades of memories for both participants and audience. Elizabeth "Liz" White was the granddaughter of Charles and Henrietta Shearer.

In August 1948, Liz White, director, addressed more than fifty members of the Open Door Club to talk up the production of *Cooling Waters*, a play about slavery she had written and staged through the Shearer Summer Theatre Negro Experimental Group. Front-page advertisements encouraged attendance at the play for a mere $1.20.

Olive Tomlinson recalled when Liz White pressed her into service as a slave in *Cooling Waters*. "We children hated anything to do with slavery," she wrote in her *Memoirs*. "It was incomprehensible that sane adults would stand on a stage, dress in slave clothing and speak slave dialogue. In retrospect these adults were not sane. They took chances. They were creative in theater, photography, and art. They were artists having a good time." The role was humiliating for Olive but earned a positive review.

Over the years, Shearer Summer Theatre performed many plays, including *Rain*, adopted from a story by Somerset Maugham (1949); *Anna Lucartas* (1952); and the highlight, *Othello* (1960).

In her *Memoirs*, Olive Tomlinson wrote of her mother, Olive "Cutie" Bowles: "She was active only when pressed into service by her friend, Liz White. It was

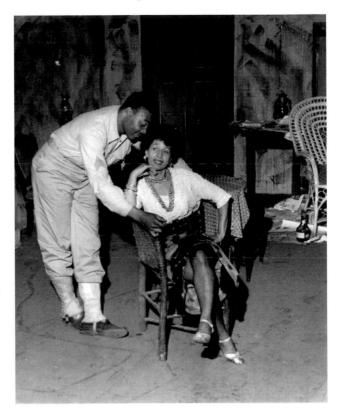

Right: Liz White is in her element on stage during a performance of *Rain* by the Shearer Summer Theatre. *Photo by William Bowles; courtesy of Olive Bowles Tomlinson.*

Below: Harry T. Burleigh posed at the Gay Head Lighthouse with Eugenia Jordan, Dorothy West and Helene Johnson (mother of Abigail McGrath) to his left, respectively. In front are John and Tom Mosely. Even in the 1930s, it was a popular place to go. *Courtesy of the Martha's Vineyard Museum.*

that friendship that involved her in Shearer Summer Theater where she was never the star, but always the feisty scene stealing second lead." Olive went on to say, "Mother was a seamstress all her life. She made the outfits for the plays." Cutie Bowles was also an accomplished artist whose paintings were recognized at Island art shows and still draw attention and admiration to this day. Olive's father, William Bowles, earned credit both for scenery construction and as cast photographer. As an aside, Olive added that her father chauffeured Harry T. Burleigh from New York to the Vineyard in the 1930s.

The high point of the Shearer Summer Theatre, clearly, was the staging of *Othello*. Cutie Bowles played Emelia and sewed her own gown. All the actresses made their own outfits. "Othello was so good, so special," said Olive. "Twin Cottages had a front porch and balcony, and we used the pathways and the top floor with a widow's walk. Grand setting. It was a labor of love in terms of everyone who took part. Liz White put it together. Did it all." She paused. "'The moor has killed thy mistress,' my mother yelled, running through the trees and the audience. Liz White wanted to film it. She did it, but it took her twenty years."

***

In the 1930s, prejudice, as noted by Dean Denniston, was prevalent on the Vineyard. Restaurants and bars refused to serve blacks. The only town on the Island willing to sell houses to African Americans was Oak Bluffs. School Street evolved into a small black community.[50] Even as more African Americans came to the Vineyard, either as summer visitors or year-round residents, the numbers were small in the 1940s. Circuit Avenue, East Chop and the Highlands had a few black families. Dr. Lucien Brown of New York bought a house that was "directly across from the beach [and] was purchased in August 1944 through the familiar technique of a 'straw' using a white intermediary who would be willing to sell to a black."[51]

"Being of color was distinctive back in the 30s on the Island,"[52] J. Riche Coleman was quoted as saying. "No one saw you. No one heard you. No one knew you. You knew it." He said, proudly, "Ours was a beautiful generation," and then recounted exploits with friends from School Street to the Highlands to the Town Pier.

Joseph Stiles (1925–2006) was born in Virginia, raised in New Jersey and stationed at the Naval Air Base on Martha's Vineyard during World War

II. He spent time on a naval ship that traveled to the South Pole, but as an African American, Mr. Stiles was relegated to culinary chores, preparing food for the officers and tidying up their living quarters. "That's as far up in the Navy a black could get at that time. Just in the kitchen."

Mr. Stiles elaborated on the prejudice:

> *I was in the Quonset huts with the rest of the colored fellows and the white soldiers was in barracks, nice warm barracks, showers and everything. In the mornings, to go wash up, take showers and things, we had to walk out of the Quonset huts and go across to the nearest barracks to shower. See, the*

"There was a lot of racists. That's why I signed up for ship duty as soon as I could." Joseph Stiles (quoted by Arthur Railton in *The History of Martha's Vineyard*, 2006) faced bigotry from the white sailors when he was stationed on Martha's Vineyard during World War II. *Photo taken in 1946, courtesy of Joyce Stiles-Tucker.*

"The Island people were great to the blacks. That's why I came here to live afterwards, because Island people always treated us beautiful." Joseph Stiles (quoted by Arthur Railton in *The History of Martha's Vineyard*, 2006). *Photo taken in 1946, courtesy of Joyce Stiles-Tucker.*

Navy was very prejudiced. The whole armed forces was very prejudiced in those days. They recognized us as a second-class force. The base here got so bad that we couldn't eat at the same table with them when we'd go for chow; it got so bad because they had a lot of boys there that was racists.

Racism was sometimes bad on the base, but it was not anywhere else on the Island; the Island people were great. That's why I came here to live, because Island people always treated us beautiful. I said, "This is the place I'm going to live in civilian life."[53]

Stiles did not encounter such racism aboard ship. The captain wouldn't tolerate it. "We were escorting merchant ships and protecting them against

German submarines," he said. Although based in Newport, his ship was sent to the Vineyard to block a German submarine off Gay Head. He later learned that the sub captain had defected. After the war, Stiles was aboard a destroyer that accompanied Admiral Byrd's expedition to the South Pole in 1946–47, known as Operation Deep Freeze.

Mr. Stiles fell in love with the Island and met and married Mary Cecilio, a Cape Verdean woman who grew up on the Vineyard. He came to Martha's Vineyard at the age of eighteen, in 1943, married Mary in 1945 and remained on Island the rest of his life, raising three children in the Island community: Joyce, Kenneth and Shari. "He liked being on Island," says Joyce. "He was here over sixty years, his whole adult life."

After his naval service, Stiles worked on fiberglass boats, again at the airport, and at Cronigs Brothers Market, then in downtown Vineyard Haven, where Off Main is now. For over twenty years, he delivered arrangements for Morrice Florist. Upon his retirement, he volunteered at the Senior Center, where his daughter Joyce is director. "He knew all there was about plants," she recalls fondly.

***

Chicago CPA Theodore Jones was on a Vineyard vacation when he decided to play a round of golf. He rented clubs for a dollar, paid his two-dollar greens fee, purchased tees and balls for three dollars and set off on the links. He had played just four holes and teed up his ball on the fifth fairway when the manager of the club approached and told Mr. Jones he had to leave the course. Immediately.

Mr. Jones took the case to court, as reported in the *Vineyard Gazette*: *Theodore Jones v. Thomas Attridge of the Martha's Vineyard Country Club*. The year was 1947. "The complaint alleges that on August 11, Mr. Attridge, being owner, operator or manager of the Martha's Vineyard Country Club, situated in Oak Bluffs, did make distinction, discrimination or restriction on account of color or race, in violation of Chapter 272, Section 98, of the General Laws and amendments." The judge denied a motion to quash the complaint.

This first racial discrimination case hinged on an ad in the *Gazette* that invited visitors and guests to play at the country club, with "a cordial welcome to all Vineyard visitors." This advertisement defined the golf course as a place of public amusement, according to Mr. Jones. The club argued that it was open only to members and guests.

"Just one more question," said Jones's attorney. "What race do you belong to?"
"I'm a Negro," was the reply."

On Friday, August 22, 1947, a decision was handed down by the judge. He found that the commonwealth could not prove discrimination had taken place beyond a reasonable doubt. Mr. Jones lost his case, even though the golf club had publicized its open invitation. Subtle discrimination was still the order of the day.

***

Years ago, Francine Kelly, as a teenager, came to the Vineyard for vacation. She recalls:

We went to the Wesley House. We had a reservation, my mother, my grandfather and my uncle. When my mother went in, the manager said, "I thought you were a doctor." My mother said, "I am a doctor." He said, "But you can't stay here. We don't take colored people here." And she said, "But I wrote you a check." He threw the $70 check at us and said, "You go down the street to the colored pugilist, Maitlands, a little yellow house." My room was on the second floor. That was 1951, and we stayed there in '52 as well.

And the reason we came here was friends said you should buy in Oak Bluffs. My mother was very stubborn. She said, "I want to buy where I have a view and I can paint." And they said, "Well you're going to have trouble." She wanted a place that overlooked Menemsha Harbor.

She paid cash for the land and she paid an architect. If she had been able to buy and build, we would have our house in Chilmark today. But they gave us back our money. We didn't come back. My mother was that stubborn. She said she was finished. And so it goes; it is what it is.

I came back with my husband in the '60s. And in '79 Jack [her husband] took a sabbatical and this man got us a house, now called the Waban House. From 1979 to 1983 we rented the house in August. They [her four daughters] grew up in their teens in those years. And then we were going to buy it, but we didn't buy it.

Janis [her daughter] always said she wanted to buy a house in that neighborhood [Waban Park] because we could walk to town and walk home and not have to ride in cars. "Never will my daughter have to get a ride home," says Janis. Janis bought it in 1990, before she was married.

I came with the idea I would eventually live here. I studied the environment to see if I could stand it. Whenever I took a vacation from Indianapolis, I would come here. I moved here in 2003.

Francine Kelly served admirably as executive director of Featherstone Center for the Arts from 2003 until her retirement in the late summer of 2010.

***

High Beach was the most popular beach in the Highlands, near the ferry slip, adjacent to the current East Chop Beach Club. As more white people moved into the area, African Americans were pushed down the shore to what became known, first derogatorily and then popularly, as the Inkwell.

Barbara Townes recalled:

I remember when they told the people who used Highland Beach that they could not use it anymore. It had been a public beach, but now they were leasing it to a group of people from East Chop. And this is what was told to us; they refused to have any black people on the beach. They decided they wanted a private beach and they said, no, they only had a few of their friends who were going to be shareholders in this beach and clubhouse.[54]

This story did not become a court case, but it is the background for what became known as the Inkwell. Dorothy West also encountered such segregation. "When we first came down here [1943] there were places— boarding houses—where colored people could stay. Black families were not welcome everywhere. At some restaurants and on certain beaches. We went to Highland Beach, but it became a 'private' beach. We were not welcome. But so much has changed."[55]

The issue of civil rights has been played across the national stage for decades. Even on Martha's Vineyard, there are inferences and connections to the national movement. And in 2010, there is room for improvement in racial harmony, although the Island, and the nation, have come a long way.

Chapter 7

CIVIL RIGHTS

C lifford Durr (1899–1975) was an Alabama attorney who represented Rosa Parks in her criminal appeal after her arrest for failure to surrender her seat to a white person in Montgomery, Alabama, in 1955.

On December 1, 1955, Rosa Parks (1913–2005), age forty-two, had worked a long day as a seamstress at Montgomery Fair, a department store, where she earned twenty-three dollars a week. Rosa Parks was a very proud woman and had volunteered her time with the NAACP to help young people with their schoolwork. She boarded the bus, a bag of groceries in her arms, and sat in the Negro section of the bus. But when more white people boarded the bus, the driver ordered her to the back of the bus, as was the custom. Rosa refused to give up her seat on a city bus to a white man. The driver called the police. Rosa was arrested for violation of the city and state segregation ordinance that required blacks to sit (or stand) at the back of the bus.

Attorney Durr defended Rosa Parks, with local Montgomery attorney Fred Gray, an African American. They bailed her out on December 2. She pled guilty to disorderly conduct and was charged ten dollars, plus court costs of four dollars. That might have been the end of the case, but Rosa was willing to put her name on the line and become a cause célèbre. Her actions eventually broke the back of segregated transportation in the South.

An earlier case, during the spring of 1955, involved Claudette Colvin, fifteen, who was pregnant and refused to give up her seat to a white man. Her case was deemed not as strong as that of Rosa Parks.

The Reverend Ralph Abernathy suggested formation of an organization to coordinate a one-day bus boycott in support of Rosa Parks. He named it the Montgomery Improvement Association. Some ten to fifteen thousand African Americans gathered on the eve of the boycott. A then little-known preacher spoke to the crowd. Reverend Martin Luther King Jr. "made a magnificent speech that electrified the black people,"[56] wrote Virginia Durr. "He became their undoubted leader that night."

There was phenomenal support for the bus boycott, which lasted not 1 but 381 days and effectively desegregated the city buses of Montgomery. During the boycott, white people who offered rides to blacks were ticketed by the police. One African American woman explained how she dealt with the anger the boycott caused among white people: "I learned one thing in my life and that is, when your hand's in the lion's mouth, it's just better to pat it on the head." Rosa Parks became the symbol of the civil rights movement, and Reverend Martin Luther King became its spokesman.

The Island connection to this famous incident is that Clifford and Virginia Durr's grandson, Fain Hackney, is an Edgartown attorney who lives in West Tisbury with his wife Melissa, also an attorney. And the Durrs' great-granddaughters, Annabelle and Lucy Hackney, are students in the Martha's Vineyard public schools. Virginia Durr spent summers with her daughter and son-in-law, Lucy and Sheldon Hackney, of Vineyard Haven.

***

A tiny item on the front page of the *Vineyard Gazette* of September 17, 1961, read, "Woollcott Smith of Lambert's Cove and East Lansing, Michigan had time for a brief sojourn on the Island, after his freedom order stay in the Mississippi State Penitentiary in Parchman, before he had to fly back to appear at the appeal of his sentence."

This innocuous piece, buried in the archives of history, deserves a deeper view. Two months prior to this casual vacation notice, the *Gazette* noted facetiously that "Woollcott Smith suffers no 'Southern Discomfort,'" under the heading "Freedom Riders Dine Together in Roanoke." The article referred to Woollcott Smith as "the Vineyard's own Freedom Rider," a member of a group of three whites and two Negroes who traveled to Tennessee, integrated a Holiday Inn and then conducted sit-ins at two other restaurants until threatened with arrest. They were denied service in both Knoxville and Chattanooga. The worst fate the Freedom Riders had suffered, to date, was the hostility of "cold glances."

Two weeks later came the arrest. Woollcott is a white man; the arrest occurred because "Woollcott Smith refused to leave the waiting room reserved for Negroes." The story detailed the bus ride from Boston to Nashville, Tennessee, and on to Jackson, Mississippi, where the arrest took place. The Freedom Ride had been organized by the Congress of Racial Equality.

Woollcott Smith is alive and well and living in West Tisbury. For a number of years he worked at the Woods Hole Oceanographic Institute as a mathematician statistician. Woollcott shared memories of his experience in jail and NAACP activities on the Vineyard nearly a half century ago.

"I spent about twenty-five days in jail in Parchman, Mississippi." Woollcott explained that between two and three hundred people were jailed for Freedom Rides that summer. He was arrested close to the end of the Rides and spent most of the month of August 1961 in jail. As a junior at Michigan State, it was an experience that has affected his whole life. "At first we were all in a mob cell, which was a large room with white male Freedom Riders. About halfway through, we were transferred to a maximum security prison with two people to a cell, with bars clanging and all."

He explained that much of his activism was spawned from his East Lansing, Michigan boyhood. Following his arrest, he went to meetings of the NAACP, but not on Martha's Vineyard, as there was no active chapter at the time. "We traveled to Cape Cod, down dark roads to a meeting house in Mashpee. It was a little strange. I remember there was a Vanderhoop from the tribe. There was joint interest and camaraderie. That was my direct involvement with the local community."

Woollcott recommends a book[57] that describes the Freedom Riders in the early summer of 1961. Their goal was to ride Greyhound buses into the Deep South, eat at segregated restaurants and desegregate interstate buses, with the goal of ending decades of segregation in public transportation. John Lewis, the current Georgia congressman and a Freedom Rider, wrote, "It was a ride meant to awaken the heart of America to the injustice of its own laws and traditions. It was a ride meant to stir the souls of the Deep South to listen to the cries of their American cousins."

A small announcement in the *Gazette* on August 16, 1963, read: "The Cottagers, a community group of Oak Bluffs, will entertain for the group of young Freedom Fighters, all college students from the South, who will be vacationing on the Island the week of August 19."

***

Reverend Martin Luther King Jr. (1929–1968) vacationed on the Vineyard. The editor of the *Gazette* sought an interview with him in 1962, but King's time was limited, as he was writing one of his most influential books, *Strength to Love*, published in 1963. He wrote a letter to the editor, still in the newspaper's files.

Martin Luther King, Jr.

Ebenezer Baptist Church

407 Auburn Avenue, N. E.

Atlanta, Georgia

Jackson 2-4395

September 17, 1961

Mr. Henry Bettle Hough, Editor
Vineyard Gazette
Martha's Vineyard, Massachusetts

Dear Mr. Hough:

This is to acknowledge receipt of your letter of August 11 which I received during my visit to Martha's Vineyard. I regret so much that circumstances made it impossible for me to comply with your request for an interview. It so happened that I spent the whole month of August working on a manuscript that should be placed in the hands of my publisher very soon. This made it impossible for me to accept many of the invitations that came to me during my month on the Island. I am sure you can understand how one finds it difficult to turn away from writing once he has started.

I hope it will be possible for me to meet you at some other time. I am deeply grateful for all of your encouraging words concerning our struggle in the south, and for the support that you gave the Montgomery Improvement Association.

Sincerely yours,

Martin Luther King, Jr.

Km

Letter from Dr. Martin Luther King Jr. to Henry Beetle Hough of the *Vineyard Gazette*. Ever the diplomat, Dr. King politely refused an interview with the preeminent editor on the Vineyard. *Courtesy of the* Vineyard Gazette.

The *Vineyard Gazette* printed Martin Luther King's "Letter from the Birmingham City Jail" of April 15, 1963: "My friends, I must say to you that we have not made a single gain in civil rights without determined legal and nonviolent pressure. History is the long and tragic story of the fact that privileged groups seldom give up their unjust posture…We know through painful experience that freedom is never voluntarily given by the oppressor; it must be demanded by the oppressed." People on the Vineyard were well aware of the activities of the civil rights movement and recognized that participants came from all walks of life.

***

"On Saturday morning at dawn, dressed as the upstanding citizens that we were (the men in slacks and blazers, and the women in dresses and low heels) we boarded the bus to the capitol." So begins Olive Tomlinson's account, in her *Memoirs*, of the historic March on Washington in August 1963. Olive rode the bus with her father, her husband Joe and friends Phyllis Breier and Patrick Sheehan.

> As we rode through Maryland we joined the hundreds of buses that were converging on the capital in a slow, steady cortege. In the fields beside the highway were Black people who stood silently and timidly waved their hands. These were country people, who looked like sharecroppers in ragged overalls, some even without shoes.
>
> Phyllis doesn't cry readily, and I've seen her cry only twice during our long friendship. With her back to us, she looked out of the window and hesitantly waved back at the people. From across the aisle, Joe said to her, "You look like the Queen waving to the crowd." Phyllis turned towards us with her eyes full of tears.
>
> The importance of the day finally began to register as we saw those people. It was made even more vivid as we approached Washington, D.C. The buses slowly streamed into the outskirts and then into the city itself where the streets were lined with soldiers and national guardsmen—a military barricade aligned shoulder to shoulder. The soldiers were very young and looked frightened.

Olive Tomlinson's portrayal of the bus ride to the March on Washington on August 28, 1963 is a symbolic summation of the entire civil rights movement.

Civil Rights

***

"It would be lacking in a sense of news," the *Gazette* observed in late summer 1963, "if nothing else, to omit the comment that Reverend Martin Luther King, Jr. whose Washington speech last week was one of the memorable aspects of the freedom march, has been a Vineyard visitor. It is true that his vacation here a year or so ago was by way of complete rest and retreat, but his presence did not go unnoticed."

In 1964, King became the youngest person awarded the Nobel Peace Prize, at thirty-five, for his leadership in the civil rights movement to end racial segregation and discrimination by promoting nonviolence as the most effective means of civil disobedience.

***

In 1964, Reverend Henry Bird, the young minister of Vineyard Haven's Grace Episcopal Church, invited Massachusetts Episcopal bishop John Burgess (1909–2003) to conduct summer Sunday services at the Chilmark Community Center. Bishop Burgess was the first African American to serve as an Episcopal bishop. In his honor, and for his efforts on behalf of African Americans, a stained-glass window was installed in Grace Church in 1999. His daughter, Julia Burgess, is the current executive director of Martha's Vineyard Community Services.

In the spring of 1964, motivated in part by the newly re-formed NAACP and by Reverend Bird, five West Tisbury women—Peg Lilienthal, Virginia Mazer, Polly Murphy, Nancy Smith and Nancy Whiting—packed two cars with food and clothing and drove down to Williamston, North Carolina. The plan was to deliver the supplies, participate in a voter registration campaign with African Americans in the community and return home.

Once the five women arrived in North Carolina, they gathered at a church in Williamston and stayed the night with individual black families. They participated in a voter registration drive the next day. The leader of the drive was unsure how to best utilize these five white ladies from Massachusetts. It was decided the group would picket against discrimination by the local Sears and Roebuck store. The women were among those arrested for picketing without a permit and jailed overnight on May 1, 1964. They produced bail and were released the next day.

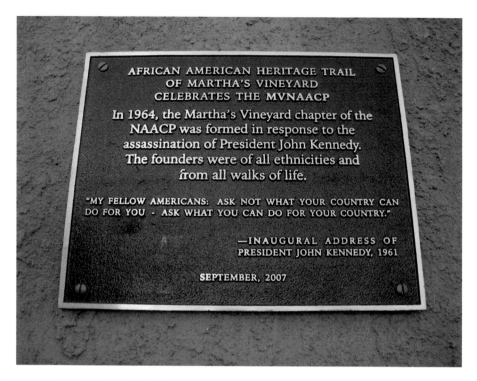

The Vineyard chapter of the NAACP was reconstituted on November 22, 1963—coincidentally, the day President Kennedy was assassinated. *Photo by Thomas Dresser.*

Forty years later, they shared their emotional travail with Linsey Lee of the Martha's Vineyard Museum. Following are some of their comments, as compiled in August 2007 in the *Dukes County Intelligencer*, a publication of the Martha's Vineyard Museum.

> *Polly Murphy: It was a very ugly situation down there, a lot of violence. Black people had difficulty registering to vote, they couldn't eat in restaurants, they were getting shot at.*
> *Nancy Whiting: It was supposed to be that we weren't going to jail. We were just going to take the food and the clothes. We knew it was dangerous. We certainly knew that. We knew we might go to jail. And we didn't know if we would come back alive.*
> *Peg Lilienthal: At the approach to Williamston, we were followed by a police cruiser. They followed us all the way into the black community where we were staying.*

Nancy Whiting: We were utterly aware that we were being watched as we came into town. Sort of the vigilante scene.

Peg Lilienthal: It was a community that was so terribly, terribly poor.

Nancy Whiting: The black people were so nice. They warmly welcomed us and fed us, and they had a church, which is where they met every night.

Virginia Mazer: When it was arranged that we would picket, we'd been out on the pavement probably five minutes before we were arrested. That was the plan. See, they needed publicity. They needed something to happen so we went to jail. We only stayed overnight, night and a day.

Polly Murphy: The whites walking by looked at us with real hate. You know, I'm sure people have disliked me from time to time, but I've never experienced hate like that...We were split up between two cells.

Virginia Mazer: What held our spirits up were the young blacks who went with us. They'd been to jail so many times they knew how.

Peg Lilienthal: Then we were bailed out, again rather hysterically—the chief of police or sheriff, whoever he was, screaming at us about barging in on Southern affairs because they'd never had any trouble with you-know-who until we came.

Virginia Mazer: We each paid five hundred dollars bail.

It was May 1, 1964, when five women from West Tisbury were arrested and jailed in Williamston, North Carolina, a brave act in a trying time. *Photo by Joyce Dresser.*

Polly Murphy: We got bailed out by our assorted husbands at home, and came out the next afternoon with the group of black people waiting to greet us, and they took us and we had a lovely dinner that they had prepared.

Nancy Smith: Back on the Vineyard, they had a big welcoming committee for us, all our children and friends were all at the dock with signs and we felt like heroes or something. Shirley Mayhew had a big supper for us and a lot of our friends were there and all our children were there and we talked. We didn't tell them how many times we got lost driving down.

Virginia Mazer: Bob Tankard was in the front of the parade [on July 4] with a flag, and curiously there was a little ripple of applause, which was so good.

Nancy Whiting: I think we felt we'd been empowered, we'd been strengthened. You were part of something. That changes your own boundaries.

Woollcott Smith, then a graduate student at Michigan State listening to his college radio station, heard that his mother had been arrested and jailed in Williamston. "It was fairly nerve wracking, especially since I had some experience in the South myself," he recalled. Once he learned the five women had been bailed out and were on their way home, he confided, "I was very proud."

***

Chris Murphy, Polly Murphy's son, recalled the atmosphere on the Vineyard in the early 1960s. "I was in high school. It was an interesting time. In retrospect things look different."

He recalled that Martha's Vineyard was very conservative at the time, but a young activist minister, Reverend Henry Bird, incited a lot of people to become involved in the NAACP and the activities of the South. Chris joined fellow high school students in what he called "a kids' version of the NAACP." He went off to Washington by bus with Bob Tankard's mother, Audria, just the two of them. "It was a big deal to see the movers and shakers. It was a real moment. A very emotional time, getting it started in the summer of '63."

Growing up in Chilmark, Chris had never met any black people. At the time, he didn't realize there was a concerted effort to deny housing to them. "I felt naive. My world was pretty limited. People at the bottom of the totem pole were either black or Native American."

Chris talked about how people view themselves. He gives credit to the Native American community, which inspired self-awareness and pride in its culture. At the same time, "the NAACP was pushing for a wider social acceptance. Now it's in the school system with people from all over; it's a new dynamic." Of his mother's trip to Williamston, he said, "They did what they did because they felt they had no choice. All they thought they were doing was taking food down, but then they did more than they wanted to. It wasn't as much as the Freedom Riders, like Woollcott integrating restaurants and riding the buses." It was not easy. Chris recalls that a friend of his mother thought the drive south should not take place, that it was none of his mother's business.

Other activities occurred on the Vineyard in that long-ago era. A busload of kids from North Carolina stayed with families on the Island; another busload came from Roxbury, and Vineyarders traveled to and fro. Chris recalled, "We picketed Louise Day Hicks, [that was] democracy on the steps of the state capital."

That he was taken seriously by the adults is what Chris recalls most. They treated the teens as partners in the process. "We sat in on their conversations, in the living rooms of their houses." It became part of his education that racial harmony was part of life, or should be.

Chris recalled a lecture he once got from an African American woman when he was dating her daughter on Island. She warned that he should be careful because of the challenges an interracial child would face. "That made me sit up," said Chris. "Yet I still had my eye on every one of Bobby Tankard's beautiful sisters!"

***

L. Joseph Overton was a union organizer in Harlem in the late 1940s and served as secretary of the Negro American Labor Council from 1960 to 1970. Overton moved to the Vineyard in 1956, and his home, Vila Rosa, was known as the "summer white house." Through the trauma of the 1960s, as the civil rights movement struggled to gain momentum, many prominent African Americans visited the Vineyard and stayed at the home of Joseph Overton, on the shores of Oak Bluffs, situated above the Inkwell beach.

Overton's guests included an array of prominent participants in the civil rights movement and beyond: Bayard Rustin, Jesse Jackson, Hulan Jack

Joseph Overton was a labor organizer in the butcher business in New York in the 1940s. On the Vineyard, he hosted civil rights leaders at his spacious house on the Oak Bluffs shore. *Photo by Joyce Dresser.*

(mayor of Harlem), Joe Louis, Dizzy Gillespie and Harry Belafonte, among others. His favorite guests were A. Philip Randolph and C.B. Powell, editor of the *Amsterdam News*.

Martin Luther King Jr. stayed at Vila Rosa. Neighbor Kathy Henderson recalled, "I remember Dr. King sitting on the Overton's deck writing, reading and discussing and he used to love the beach, but we never bothered him. We gave him space, and he didn't seem to be asking for any special attention."

That so many important people visited the Vineyard through the invitation of Joe Overton made Vila Rosa a special site on the African American Heritage Trail. When the house was dedicated in 2004, Dr. Elaine Cawley Weintraub recognized "the love that the former owners of the property, the Overton family, had for their family, friends and for Martha's Vineyard."

Chapter 8

SOCIAL ACTIVISTS

The National Association for the Advancement of Colored People was founded in 1909 in response, in part, to violence against African Americans in lynchings and a race riot in Springfield, Illinois. A number of white liberals, and some blacks, were instrumental in its creation, and it is the oldest and largest civil rights organization in the country, with more than half a million members.

Initially, the specific goal of the NAACP was to ensure that citizens are protected by the Thirteenth, Fourteenth and Fifteenth Amendments of the United States Constitution, which guarantee abolition of slavery, equal protection under the law and universal suffrage, or the right to vote. It was primarily focused on African Americans. Today, the intent of the organization is to ensure the protection of civil rights for all citizens.

The first chapter of the NAACP on the Vineyard was founded in 1931, but it languished for many years. In fact, during the early 1960s, there was no functioning chapter. Several Vineyarders, black and white, gathered on November 22, 1963, and reconstituted the Vineyard chapter of the NAACP. The group felt that it had to pursue the original mission. In the words of Nancy Whiting, "That was when we voted into existence a branch of the NAACP here. We went ahead and did it that day, even though he [John F. Kennedy] had been assassinated, thinking that was an appropriate thing to do on that day."[58] She explained that the makeup of the initial group consisted of "an odd mix, us good liberal kids, a few blacks—the Tankards were very involved—the clergy and some people from the Jewish community."

The rector of Grace Church, Henry Bird, had been in contact with the Southern Christian Leadership Conference and was instrumental in orchestrating the West Tisbury 5 to make the drive to Williamston, North Carolina, in May 1964. The link between the NAACP and other civil rights organizations has been an integral strength of the African American community, although the NAACP generally has opted for a more conservative route over the years.

Each year the Vineyard chapter of the NAACP gathers to recognize the efforts of Dr. Martin Luther King Jr. It's a chance for self-analysis, to see the progress made in the civil rights movement and acknowledge the work still to be done. In 1990, Paula Delbonis reported in the *Gazette* on the annual NAACP function in honor of Dr. Martin Luther King Jr. Over half of the Island's three hundred members were in attendance, and the guest speaker, Dr. James Comer, a prominent Yale child psychiatrist, spoke on the role of education in the African American experience.

Dr. Comer discussed African Americans in comparison to other immigrant groups. Uniquely, African Americans lost their cultural identity. "The period of slavery left the black people with a sense of dependence and inadequacy and no sense of a better future." Dr. Comer expounded on the problem: "The negative psychological and social consequence for many were transmitted from one generation to another. During the time when America was preparing for the post industrial society, from 1900–1940, most blacks were being deprived of education." As an educator, a psychiatrist and an African American, Dr. Comer has a perceptive view of the challenges faced by African Americans.

Personally, Dr. Comer noted that he and his four siblings have thirteen college degrees among them. His situation is unusual. He felt that African Americans have been seriously neglected in the realm of education and that has had a very detrimental effect on their lives.

In 1993, the NAACP dinner again celebrated the life of Dr. Martin Luther King Jr.[59] Dr. Milton Mazer (Virginia's husband) received an award and gave a short speech. He recalled the early days of the Vineyard chapter of the NAACP, when members wanted to participate in protests against racism. They went South "and to jail," he said. "We had rallies. We marched in the Edgartown Fourth of July parade. We remembered that the church bells rang the day when President Johnson passed the Civil Rights bill."

The mission of the Martha's Vineyard chapter of the NAACP recognizes the power of education and the importance of cultural heritage. The NAACP has a goal to promote an inclusive environment and maintain respect for the values and diversity of the entire Island community. Education is key to opening that environment for the benefit of all students. The specific aim is to promote and protect every citizen's civil rights, not just black, but Wampanoag, Jewish, Brazilian and white people.

Laurie Perry-Henry, president of the Vineyard chapter of the NAACP, noted in 2010 that the local chapter "has a wide span of influence, dealing with health issues and the police, involved with high school scholarships." She added, "We serve on the school search committees and have input on the school curriculum. We are all inclusive. Very effective." She paused and then added, "Civil rights is our niche."

Like most Vineyard nonprofits, the local chapter of the NAACP spends energy conducting fundraising activities in the summer, when the Island population swells to over 100,000 people. In the off-season, the group still gathers for an annual dinner to honor Dr. Martin Luther King Jr. "People like that," says Mrs. Perry-Henry. "They like the social aspect, have a cocktail and dinner." The general membership meeting takes place monthly.

***

For years, Dorothy West wrote a weekly column in the *Vineyard Gazette* that reported on local events in Oak Bluffs. Her "Cottagers Corner" column opened the eyes of white people on the Vineyard to see a vibrant African American community in their midst. One of Dorothy's pet projects was the Cottagers Club, a charitable organization of African American women who contributed to the community. And each activity was duly documented in the *Vineyard Gazette*.

Liz White, director of the Shearer Summer Theatre, was elected the president of the Cottagers Club when it was founded in 1956. Their first gift was to the Martha's Vineyard Hospital, when thirty women each chipped in ten dollars to make up a sizable contribution.

An early fundraiser was a square dance held at Shearer Cottage. Then a teenager, Olive Tomlinson recalls, "We were the youngest square, the most motivated, and of course, the winners. A half century later we still relive our triumph." The Cottagers are known for holding gala events that spark participation by the African American community.

At the end of the summer of 1957, Dorothy West reported that the Cottagers Club was "well entrenched," and the following year it had concluded its "third successful season." By 1961, it had raised enough money to grant a scholarship of fifty dollars to a needy high school graduate.

Dorothy West kept the group on the radar screens of the Island community. The name of the group originated with the name Cottage City; that was what Oak Bluffs was called when it separated from Edgartown in 1880.

The Cottagers fundraiser to benefit the young Freedom Fighters in 1963 evolved into a program four years later that celebrated "the rich cultural and historical heritage of the American Negro–often tear-stained, but not without its joy and humor," by a group called Voices, Inc., which honored the proud heritage of the African American.

By 1968, the Cottagers were financially solvent enough to purchase a building on Pequot Avenue to host their activities and fundraisers. A decade later, in August 1977, Dorothy West recounted the financial success of the Cottagers when she wrote, "Very recently the Cottagers held a mortgage burning, there being no better use for the money received from the sale of one piece of property than paying off the mortgage of the other." The Cottagers had purchased a building on Wamsutta Avenue and sold it to back the town for use as the Senior Center, operated by the Council on Aging. They used the proceeds from that sale to pay off the mortgage on the old town hall, which they had purchased in 1968. That building is now known as Cottagers Corner.

Miss West's column, "Cottagers Corner," kept the name of the group in the headlines. "They endeavor to promote and support worthwhile charitable and educational purposes which will enhance the quality of living for the Island community." The group has followed this precept for the past thirty-five years, it was noted. The Cottagers made a concerted effort to address the issue of black pride among teenagers. In 1992, their show, *WEATOC (We're Educators—A Touch of Class)*, targeted teens to bring them a sense of pride.

To raise funds, the Cottagers organize an annual summer house tour and a fashion show. These popular events draw an ever-expanding crowd and make the limited membership, capped at one hundred women, a coveted position.

In honor of their fiftieth anniversary, in 2006, the Cottagers' commemorative booklet invoked their focus on "improving the Vineyard community." It went on to explain that "the Cottagers is a philanthropic organization of African American women homeowners on Martha's Vineyard." A plaque was placed on the building on Pequot Avenue, marking Cottagers Corner as an integral part of the African American Heritage Trail on Martha's Vineyard.

Dorothy West promoted the Cottagers, an energetic group of Oak Bluffs female homeowners who donate time and money for the good of their locale. Since 1956, they have instilled a sense of pride in the African American community. *Photo by Joyce Dresser.*

At their gala celebration, Dr. James Comer, who addressed the NAACP back in 1990, commented that "the future of each child in the African American community and any society is determined by support." And the Cottagers have always taken a strong stance in support of education and encouragement of student success.

A second speaker, Professor Paula Giddings of Smith College, addressed the crowd. Professor Giddings, a graduate of Howard University, has researched the lives of African American women and written two defining books on social history: *When and Where I Enter: The Impact of Black Women on Race and Sex in America* and *In Search of Sisterhood: Delta Sigma Theta and the Challenge of the Black Sorority Movement*. Her latest book, *Ida: A Sword Among Lions, Ida B. Wells and the Campaign Against Lynching* (2008), is an outstanding biography on a late nineteenth-century unsung heroine of African American and women's rights.

Coming of age in the 1960s, Ms. Giddings was inspired by the Freedom Riders and wondered where they got the courage to undertake such brave efforts. At the same time, she questioned why some people felt such hatred. Ms. Giddings often visits the Vineyard with family and friends. Her aunt, Mabelle Thompson, has long extolled her literary contributions.

Mycki Jennings of New Haven, Connecticut, a faithful Cottager, was quoted in the *Gazette*: "The Cottagers have provided a way to give back to the community and to tap Cottagers' connections to make improvements in her mainland community, reducing the 6 degrees of separation to maybe 3 or 4." The *Gazette* defined the group as "a philanthropic organization of African American women, homeowners on the Vineyard…It is dedicated to giving monetary assistance to various Island causes."

Daughters of the Cottagers, a second generation of summer people, performed at the Oak Bluffs Historical Commission. They presented an enthusiastic rendition of musical compositions. The Cottagers keep on keeping on, leaving a very positive imprint on the community.

***

From July 4 to Labor Day, gathering at 7:30 each morning, a group of African American women and men celebrate the dawn of a new day. Robert Hayden wrote, "The Polar Bears represent a unique recreational, social and even spiritual experience on the Island, as the swimmers commune with nature while most of the Island is still asleep or just waking up."[60]

Social Activists

Estella Rowe of Louisville, Kentucky, who celebrated her sixtieth birthday with a visit to the Vineyard after driving up the East Coast, wrote:

As an African American, I am always particularly interested in the roles that African Americans play in our society, both past and present. We passed the Inkwell Beach along Beach Road [which] has been traditionally known as a meeting place for African American families and visitors. When we first arrived and on our way to Madison Inn, an African American woman walking our way provided us with information about the Polar Bear Club that met at the Inkwell Beach. She said her grandmother shared that the Inkwell originated with a group of African American men who met there each day to share information, camaraderie, and perhaps tall tales. My husband and I got up early one morning and went to the Inkwell Beach to observe the Polar Bear Club. I met the most wonderful group of middle age African American women who invited me to join them in the water.

This looks almost like an inkwell, with beautiful shades of black, paddling and floating in the water. The Polar Bears, as the group is affectionately known, enjoy the early morning chilly waters. The group came into existence about 1945. *Photo by Estella Rowe.*

"I found the women of the Polar Bear Club to be fascinating, courageous and intriguing because [they were] around my age. I believe that the African American gentlemen of the Polar Bear Club were of retirement age. What a spectacular way to spend one's golden years." *From left*: Eleanor Hughes, Caroline Hunter, Estella Rowe, Bernice Ryner and Janice Queen. *Photo and caption by Estella Rowe.*

I did observe a few men with the Polar Bear Club swimming, but it wasn't all about swimming for the women. I believe an invigorating, inspirational morning plunge might be a better description for the women. The women joined hands, walked into the cold water and formed a circle about ten to twenty feet off the shore. It warmed my soul to hear them singing songs together. I took a picture of the ladies in the water and because I was a distance away, and it was dawn, the shadows of ladies in the water appear to be different shades of black, like an inkwell. I would have liked to have learned more about the women I met that day. Did they live on the Vineyard, did they visit several months in the summer, did they have family who live there, were they dignitaries, politicians, artists, writers?

Mrs. Rowe concluded with an observation about Oak Bluffs as "a charming small town, a wonderful, relaxing, interesting destination." She added, "I found the people to be very friendly."

Chapter 9

FRIENDS AND FAMILY

M y sister and Adelaide Cromwell were good friends," says Mabelle Thompson, a former New York teacher. "They both attended Smith College in the late 1930s and were counselors at Camp Atwater. Adelaide was my counselor at Camp Atwater, in my early years as a camper." Mabelle went to Atwater, and when she and her husband purchased property on the Vineyard in 1971, she reconnected with many of those friends again.

"At that time [1937], nothing was integrated so it [Camp Atwater] became one of the camps to service black youth. Atwater had quite an elite clientele." Mabelle attended camp for ten years with the children of doctors, lawyers and teachers. "And that's when I first heard of the Vineyard," she smiles. "For me, it changed my life."

Mabelle and Sam Thompson first came to the Vineyard in 1956. "My uncle Walter, a playboy party-guy, used to come to the Vineyard with his wife and his girlfriend. They were all friends." Mabelle and Sam visited Uncle Walter. "Later that summer we came to Shearer Cottage for a week. We partied, got stuck in the sand, rode bikes to Edgartown. We had a good time."

Mabelle's father was grand master of the Masons of New York. He was a humble man but expected his children to do well. The Masons, like the church, offered a network for African Americans that helped with both social and economic issues because blacks "couldn't get in other organizations." Mabelle and Sam knew Joseph Overton, the labor organizer; they knew Harry T. Burleigh. Mabelle's Uncle Walter was friends with Adam Clayton Powell. Powell, Hazel Scott and Jimmy Lunceford all lived in Parkway Gardens in Greenburgh, New York.

Spencer and David Thompson, the son and his father, enjoy Tashmoo Beach in the summer of 2009. *Courtesy of Mabelle Thompson.*

Fishing off the Observation Deck at Memorial Wharf in Edgartown is an exhilarating experience for these young men. *Courtesy of Mabelle Thompson.*

Friends and Family

Mabelle Thompson's grandson Spencer Thompson and cousin Nicole Williamson, both age four, caper on the beach. *Photo taken in 1998, courtesy of Mabelle Thompson.*

And then, like many people, the Thompsons returned to the Vineyard to visit friends. "They had two kids, we had four," says Mabelle, "and we would come over first, just for the weekend, with the car loaded, lasagnas and kids. We liked it so much we started renting a house." After several years, a realtor showed them a house to buy. Mabelle says, "I remember standing in the kitchen, laughing, saying this is crazy. We had no intention of buying a house. We went back to our friends and I had two Harvey Wallbangers and Sam said, 'You want to buy that house?' Next morning we gave the realtor $200." The Thompsons have owned their Oak Bluffs house for forty years.

On the last day of school, Mabelle recalls, "We threw the kids in the car and we came here. It was just a breeze in the summer. My kids were all swimmers. They just had the time of their life. They could ride this Island with bicycles, hitch rides, dive for coins in the Oak Bluffs harbor. We were water people from the get go. They love the Island." Sam Thompson was a "boat father," coming up for the weekends from his salesman's job with Liggett-Myers Tobacco Company (Chesterfield, L&Ms, Lark). It was a perfect lifestyle for a family with four teenagers. The boys had summer jobs, made connections with friends and spent a lot of time at the beach.

"I remember when we first came here," says Mabelle, "and you had to go to the Fives to Sevens, cocktail parties galore. I finally got fed up, for we had to leave the beach, do the hair, have different decent clothes, and finally I said the hell with it." There were other memorable times too. "It's great that we reconnected with a lot of people. But the black middle class was very small; it was easy to know them on the East Coast. And I renewed all my old friendships from the '30s and '40s."

On the Vineyard, Mabelle has never faced racial challenges, although her children have. "I remember they wouldn't go to Papa Johns because someone was rude to them. They boycotted one of the pizza places. I'm not sure if it was because they were black or whether they were just off-Islanders. The Island kids were and still are some of their best friends."

Once Mabelle retired from her New York teaching position and the boys were on their own, she and Sam moved to the Vineyard. "We always kind of fell into things; we never planned anything," says Mabelle. "We've just been one of the luckiest couples in the world. As far as I'm concerned, I'm living in paradise. I can't believe it."

***

Bob Tankard and Tom Bennett have been friends for years—fifty years, give or take. They met in high school and bonded over a sense of not being accepted or appreciated, but then turned their lives around to be success stories and models of the community. Bob is black and Tom is white, but their conversation reveals an awareness that the difference in race is less important than the friendship that developed in their trust and respect for each other and how they face the world.

> *Bob Tankard: I was born in Roselle, New Jersey, one of ten children of George and Audria Tankard. I can remember coming to the Vineyard in June of 1961; I was fifteen years old and I wanted to play professional baseball.*
>
> *You have to realize that in the 1940s and '50s there were not many opportunities for African Americans in our society. Growing up in the inner city of Newark, New Jersey, one did not see many professional African Americans. I can't remember seeing an African American judge, lawyer, banker or many teachers. Jackie Robinson was the first black man I saw on a TV commercial. My mother was a black vaudeville dancer with Josephine*

Baker. My father sang at the Apollo Theater in New York. He was quite the singer and won a few contests; they used to call him Little Cab Callaway.

My mother came across an article in the Amsterdam News *about Cape Cod. She fell in love with the song by Patti Page, "Old Cape Cod," which led her to seek out this place with the sandy dunes and salty air. Once she came to the Vineyard, she knew this was the place to bring her family.*

When I came here in 1959, I went to the Inkwell, where there was a black population that came to the Vineyard every summer. The people I met there used to talk about going to prep school, going to college, becoming doctors and lawyers. I said to myself, they couldn't be serious. During that summer I realized that there were many professional African Americans who came to the Vineyard, and they were preparing their kids for college and the future. It was a strong middle class who entertained the likes of Adam Clayton Powell, Martin Luther King, Dorothy West and many more. I realized I didn't have to be a baseball player in order to be successful.

The natives accepted us with open arms, but the summer elite had problems with us because my father was a truck driver and not a professional.
Tom Bennett: You say you didn't fit in to the elite. There was classism there. There is classism within the race.
Bob Tankard: Tom became a friend because he played football. He was from Edgartown and the kids in each town didn't associate with each other. Tom and I became close because we used to talk about personal things. We bonded more quickly because we didn't have fathers around all of the time.
Tom Bennett: There was commonality between us. I had a stepfather, but it wasn't the same.
Bob Tankard: We leaned on each other's strengths. I knew Tom wanted to be something. Let me tell you a story. I went over to his house one day and I found a book named Word Power Made Easy.
Tom Bennett: He found my Word Power Made Easy *book. Used ten new words a week.*
Bob Tankard: I said to myself, what's Tom trying to score on me? I acted totally cool. The whole day we were together, that's the only thing I could think about. I remembered it for years to come.

Tom and I talked a lot about race and being underprivileged. I knew there were similarities and I realized Tom had experienced the same kind of discrimination I had.
Tom Bennett: It's interesting, too, that there's a lot of Islanders in Oak Bluffs and the rest of the Vineyard who have that attitude toward the Islanders from Edgartown. Many people think the people who grew up in

Edgartown are prejudiced, but mostly the Edgartown local folks were the ones who experienced classism, because they're the people who worked for the wealthy.

The wealthy had the yacht club, golf course and tennis courts for their kids, but local kids couldn't go there. We worked from age ten on and that way we brought money home to help support the family. The work ethic was a major value growing up.

Bobby went through that discrimination right here in Oak Bluffs. In Edgartown these clubs used to exclude blacks and Jewish people. But local people were excluded too. These were all interesting dynamics. Thankfully, all these things are changing now for the better.

Bob Tankard: As the years went on, dating was probably the hardest thing for me, because there weren't enough African American girls, girls of color, on the Island. In those days, you dated within your thing [race]. I said, this is crazy. You longed for summer, because more girls would come down.

Any time I was around Tom, I never felt I was around a white guy. I felt I was around a guy. Race wasn't an issue between us.

It was a struggle, it definitely was a struggle. I could list four or five parents I could say were openly racist at the time. And their kids, although they hung with us, would, from time to time, indicate something. You could sense it.

Tom Bennett: Even though I grew up in Edgartown, which was against the blacks and the Jews, I felt prejudice. It wasn't a prejudice of racism, when I was growing up, it was classism.

After both young men graduated from Martha's Vineyard Regional High School, class of '64, Bob joined the army in October 1964; Tom enlisted in the Air Force in January 1965. Vietnam was looming on the horizon, but neither man served there.

Tom Bennett: I grew up experiencing some prejudices, but nothing like what was to come. I learned later on, when I was in the service and stationed in Alabama, when Martin Luther King marched on Montgomery, what prejudice could do to people. I was in a room that the "domestic" black folk cleaned for the officers. We were allowed to watch the march on TV, and I saw the response from the black women of tears and hugging and the emotion, seeing them feel so much. It had an incredible impact on me. At the Capital Building in Montgomery, I saw the confederate flag flying first and the American flag flying below it.

I was on a train that went from Texas to Alabama. When we stopped, I went into this black restaurant, sat there, didn't know why they weren't waiting on me and realized I was sitting at the wrong counter and had to go right next door. And they're all looking at me, black and white, like I'm stupid. So I learned about it firsthand.

Bob Tankard: It was like that in the service. We were stationed in Fort Jackson, South Carolina. And it was one of the first times I'd seen the really down-home racist people you had to be with. They would make slurs, because they could. And when they ran into a northern guy that didn't accept that, they were like, shocked.

And there was a time we went roller-skating and we went to the rink and as we approached the door in our uniforms, the window got full of faces. How dare you guys come in here.

After three years in the service, Bob finished his tour of duty. He chose not to reenlist but didn't know what to do next. He had met people in the army who helped him decide that college was the right direction for him. When he entered college, he never looked back and went on to earn his master's and then his doctorate in education leadership and change.

Bob Tankard: I met four or five black officers, talking about the old times. They said [to me], "You need to go to school." All of them had gone to Howard or Morgan or one of the prominent black universities in the South. They said, "You're a young black man, you need to get yourself an education, make something of yourself." I realized I wanted to go back to school and work with kids.

I was in the right place at the right time [at UMass]. Because of my experience with Tom I didn't have the anger. I was able to carry myself a little different, and doors opened for me a little quicker than for other guys.

I always said, when you have someone close to you, you just take it for granted that they're there for you. I knew I could always come back when I needed brotherly love. Tom and I had this bond. We could sit down and talk. He was there for me.

Tom Bennett: I think it gets back to the absence of fathers in our lives, in a meaningful way. We had to have some kind of role model. So we became each other's role model.

Bob Tankard: I had my bachelor's degree and he was talking about a master's program. I knew I wanted to be a principal, so I went back to school. When I got my master's, Tom was working on his master's.

Tom Bennett: It was at Antioch, now Cambridge College. It was a master's program for people already working in the field of human services who needed to advance their degrees. I did the master's while I was director of summer projects, part of Community Services [on Martha's Vineyard].
Bob Tankard: I knew as an African American to go into consulting I needed a doctorate. What are you going to do to buckle your knees? I must say rigorous academics made me more committed and humble. Being an athlete you can be very cocky, and you need something to bring you back to earth. That did it, made me realize it. When I got it [the doctorate], *it really wasn't a celebration for anyone except me.*
Tom Bennett: We celebrated by going to dinner at the Yacht Club, where I am now a member. This represents how some of the old ways are changing.
Bob Tankard: Again, it was the support from family and friends that kept me going.

Beyond college degrees for both men, there was the work environment on the Vineyard. While Bob moved from teacher and coach to principal, Tom stayed within the same organization, Community Services, but his role evolved over the years.

Bob Tankard: I think of that experience [interview to be an elementary school principal] *as pain. I went through this interrogation. There was racism. The names I was called behind my back by people I had to work with, it was unbelievable.*
Tom Bennett: I think some of that was racism. But I think some of that was classism. I think a lot of people who go to private schools never accept anyone who is educated the way you and I were educated.
Bob Tankard: What was never clear to me was, where's this coming from? I feel like I'm in Montgomery, Alabama, in the '60s. I had a tape of the Jackie Robinson story. Branch Rickey told Jackie, you're going to have to put up with name-calling and indecent situations. They're looking for the least little weakness they can find.

[One antagonist] *came to me before I retired. She said, "I was one of the people who didn't want you here." I said, "I know that." She said, "I did everything in my power to keep you from getting this job." I said, "I know that." "I undermined you in every way I could." I said, "I know that." She said, "You knew all that and you provided me every opportunity to be successful."*

I said, "It's not about you and me, it's about those kids."

And all of a sudden, it was like Niagara Falls. She said, "I don't want you to go. She did a 360."

I said, "It's a team. We all got to be rolling in the same direction."

Eventually, those that were opposed were sorry.

Tom Bennett: They came around once they got to know you.

Now in their mid-sixties, Bob and Tom pause to take stock of their roles in the community, their legacy, their family and the depth of appreciation for the support they've offered each other through the years. It's not always been an easy road, but it certainly was smoother having each other's support and friendship.

Tom Bennett: I've been at Community Services forty years. My title now is associate executive director/senior clinical advisor, which evolved into a job I really like. I used to be the program director of the Mental Health Center. I see combat veterans, families and work in the community. So I'm not bored.

The thing about human service work, psychotherapists' work, experience makes a huge difference. The more experience you have, usually, translates into wisdom about human behavior. You get better at your work as you get older. It's one of the few jobs where you're more valuable the older you get, as long as your mind is still good.

Bob Tankard: I'm on the school committee. I have the television show. I'm a trustee at the bank. When you choose to be on something versus having to be something, it's different. I can't sit around.

Tom Bennett: Bob is more gregarious than I am. That's one of the words I got from my Word Power Made Easy *book.*

Bob Tankard: I had a job where I had to be more outgoing. I had to overcome a speech impediment, I stuttered. I'd talk so fast, making sure I didn't stutter, but people couldn't understand what I said. So I had to clear that up. I never thought I would have a TV show or get up in front of people and speak.

Tom Bennett: We had this understanding of how we could overcome certain things you have no control over, like being born out of wedlock, or what color you are. Some people don't like you because of those two things. I think there's a connection, which makes us a little more sophisticated about some things.

The other reason that makes us so close is that we have that unconditional positive regard for each other. We help each other to do the right thing, but if we make mistakes, that doesn't change how we feel about each other.

Bob Tankard: When you have a friend who can say to you, you messed up, and you still care for that person, it is a friendship that has been built over time and trust.

Tom Bennett: Bobby came from a matriarchal family. I grew up in a matriarchal family. So we had that influence growing up that was very similar.

Bob Tankard: Married thirty-seven years. We're in the top 1 percent.

Tom Bennett: We're very much involved with the community, and the wives have to pick up the slack. We are two very lucky men to be with the women we married. They had to put up with an awful lot from us.

Bob Tankard: You know I coached football nine years and Donna came to every Island and off-Island game.

Tom Bennett: I've been on-call I don't know how many years. We had three boys and a niece and nephew we brought up. Bobby had two girls and two stepchildren.

Bob Tankard: We have a better sense of what women's needs are than guys who weren't around women.

Tom Bennett: And we learned how to listen to what a woman has to say.

***

"Take a chair," Betty Rawlins offers upon entering the solarium of her Oak Bluffs home. She has two chairs, one awarded to her when she retired as chairman of the board of trustees of Salem State College and the second for her retirement as a member of the faculty and associate dean of the college and coordinator of the human service program at Simmons College. Her husband Keith has the rocker; the armchair is free.

In 1993, Betty and Keith Rawlins moved to the Vineyard year-round after they had resided in Hingham for twenty years. "We were statistics in town, racial statistics." They first visited friends on the Island in the 1960s, then bought a campground cottage in the 1970s. Subtle, unpleasant experiences, and the proximity of their neighbors, led them to purchase their current abode close to town in 1976. "This is the way it ought to be," their daughter said as they settled in to their new home.

Betty intended to write a children's book, "more than your typical 'color me brown' stories of white children with brown faces." It hasn't happened yet. Instead, both Betty and Keith are deeply entrenched in searching out their genealogical heritage. As the only surviving family members of their respective generation, now in their ninth decade, they are driven to uncover their past to share with their children, grandchildren and extended family.

The first part was easy. Both Betty's and Keith's paternal sides were from Barbados. Keith's grandfather knew Betty's father and provided him with housing when he first arrived in the States. It proved a challenge to discover much in Barbados other than baptism and marriage records. At his father's funeral, a man introduced himself to Keith as his cousin; that got Keith interested in his genealogy.

"I found my grandfather from North Carolina," Keith smiles. As a retired social worker, he knows the key elements to building strong family bonds. "I never knew anyone in my grandfather's family, yet he had nine siblings and two lived in Cambridge, but we never connected." He says, "Slaves only had first names. Census records show the slaves of the master, with age, but no last name." Keith learned that his ancestors were held by masters named Wortham and Reavis, and his ancestors assumed those names. "We looked through the census in Raleigh, North Carolina, to get their names," he said. He found that his great-grandmother was a Cherokee Indian, a woman he recalls fondly from his youth. "Her first name and age match, so we take it that is the name of the relative." Keith traced his mother's family back to Stephen Reavis, born in 1845.

Recently, Betty made an impressive discovery. She traced her great-great-great-grandparents back prior to 1800, out in Williamstown, Massachusetts. "You can't believe this," she says. "It's so exciting for me."

Cato Dunsett of Stamford, Connecticut, served in the Revolutionary War, and both he and, later, his wife received a pension for his military service. Betty found publication of their marriage bans for March 5, 1786. Zube, or Azabia, Prat was born in 1759 in Pelham, Massachusetts. Cato and Zube had four children: Cato Jr., born in 1790; Achsah in 1792; Roxa in 1793; and Anson in 1795.

Anson Dunsett was Betty's ancestor. His daughter, Henrietta, married Peter Hawkins, who fought for the North as a quartermaster sergeant in the Civil War. After his death, Henrietta Hawkins received a pension of eight dollars a month; Betty has a copy she received from the National Archives.

"It's really been fascinating," she says. The Rawlinses have shared the research with their children, Pattie and Paul, and grandchildren Sharisse and Keith. Learning about their ancestry through ancestry.com has given Betty and Keith Rawlins a fresh look at their past and established a firm foundation in the present.

And in the small-world department, Betty has been friends with Adelaide Cromwell for ages. "Adelaide and I have known each other since I was eighteen. She's a wonderful person. So friendly and outgoing. I really look up to her."

***

Whether family or friend, the relationships developed over the course of a lifetime prove to be the cornerstone to a healthy peace of mind. Racial slurs and antagonism have been a part of life for generations and will not disappear overnight. But the strength of a lasting friendship or relationship can overcome some of the pain inflicted by careless, callous or cruel words.

Chapter 10

HERITAGE TRAIL

When Virginia Suwannee perished in a traumatic house fire in the late spring of 1940, her death brought to an end the physical stigma of slavery in Oak Bluffs. Ms. Suwannee was born a slave, and her life represented the struggle and strife to attain a goal of self-sufficiency recognized by those around her.

For half a century, Ms. Suwannee lived and worked in Oak Bluffs as a cook, a laundress, a domestic. Born and reared in the South, she smoked a pipe and kept to herself, and she died destitute. There were no funds, as the *Gazette* put it, for "the grave of this familiar old colored mammy of slavery days," but a service was offered, with Reverend Denniston presiding, and a grave marker donated.

Fast-forward fifty years. Martha's Vineyard Regional High School history teacher Elaine Cawley Weintraub was discussing the early history of the Vineyard. She fielded a question from one of her students: "Where were the black people then?"

That question inspired Dr. Weintraub to link up with Carrie Tankard of the NAACP, and together they began an exhaustive study of African Americans on Martha's Vineyard. Out of their research was born the African American Heritage Trail of Martha's Vineyard, which has become an exemplary story expounding on the influence and impact African Americans have made on Martha's Vineyard over the past three centuries.

Early in 1996, $1,000 was raised to begin work on the trail, and by the annual Martin Luther King Jr. birthday function in January 1997, Dr. Weintraub and Ms. Tankard distributed a booklet they had prepared that outlined primary sites for the African American Heritage Trail. It was a major step, giving historical significance to specific places around the Island that had played a role in African American history. The Trail Committee reported sales of between four and five thousand booklets. Shearer Cottage was the first site where a plaque was dedicated on the trail, in late summer 1997. Over the years, high school students under Dr. Weintraub's jurisdiction have commemorated nearly two dozen additional sites on the Vineyard, with a plaque on site and publicity in the press. Students have learned how African Americans played an integral role in the history of Martha's Vineyard; this gives them a broader view of their past and their present.

In the spring of 1998, high school students cleared undergrowth and trash from the neglected Eastville Cemetery by the Lobster Hatchery in Oak Bluffs. Dr. Weintraub and her students placed a plaque in the cemetery, recognizing that it had served as a final resting spot for "mariners, vagrants and people of color."

It is conceivable that Rebecca Michael, daughter of Nancy Michael, was buried at the Eastville Cemetery, as it is close to where Jeremiah Pease lived. There is now a bench and a plaque bearing Rebecca Michael's name. A

This view of Shearer Cottage is from the Baptist Temple Park. Shearer is a well-run, popular inn steeped in African American tradition, conveniently located in the Highlands, not far from downtown Oak Bluffs. *Photo by Joyce Dresser.*

plaque was also installed at Memorial Wharf in Edgartown to acknowledge Nancy Michael, Rebecca's mother, the woman known as Black Nance.

Pulpit Rock, where John Saunders is said to have exhorted African Americans in the Farm Neck community of Oak Bluffs, was dedicated in 1999. Because of ownership issues, the plaque was placed on adjacent Land Bank property.

Funds from the Massachusetts Cultural Council were used to produce a map of the African American Heritage Trail in January 2000. In the autumn of that year, Dr. Weintraub celebrated the Landladies, two boardinghouses on Lower Circuit Avenue. Louisa Izett and Georgia O'Brien provided lodging to African Americans who were denied accommodation at white-only hotels. Louisa Izett is listed in the 1907 Resident Directory of Oak Bluffs as the owner of the residence at 220 Circuit Avenue; we can assume that her boardinghouse was open. Room and board, at the time, was seven dollars per week. Today, the rates are higher, but Tivoli Inn on Circuit Avenue is still open for business. A bench in nearby Hiawatha Park honors these courageous, enterprising sisters.

The Heritage Trail branched out of town in 2001 to recognize Randall Burton, the fugitive slave who escaped from Chilmark to New Bedford in the

This bench bears a dedication to the women who ran boardinghouses for African Americans when no other inns, besides Shearer Cottage, accepted African American guests. "African American Heritage Trail celebrates the landladies of Oak Bluffs. Because of them, people of color were able to live, work and vacation here." *Photo by Joyce Dresser.*

autumn of 1854. Two plaques were erected, one in the West Basin and the other in Menemsha itself, indicating the route Mr. Burton traversed.

Edward W. Brooke's "home was a social center of a group of people of affluence and education, who created their own Vineyard summer community," said Dr. Weintraub at the dedication of the Brooke house on Nashawena Avenue in Oak Bluffs in October 2003. Edward W. Brooke was the first African American state attorney general in the country (1963–66) and the first African American United States senator (1967–78) elected since the days of Reconstruction. The Suffolk County Juvenile Courthouse in Boston now bears the name Edward W. Brooke Courthouse.

By 2004, the Heritage Trail had obtained another grant from the Massachusetts Foundation for the Humanities to expand its book, which included additional sites on the route. The new tome, entitled *Lighting the Trail*, represents a dozen years of research by Dr. Weintraub. In her review of the book, Della Hardman commended Dr. Weintraub on leading the research into probated wills and the background of the Landladies' cottages and promoting murals painted at the high school in recognition of African American events on the Vineyard.

Cottagers Corner, the former town hall, was dedicated in July 2006. This honored the Cottagers in their organization of a philanthropic social group of African American women, as well as the efforts of Dorothy West, whose weekly newspaper column was appreciated over the years.

A site was dedicated to commemorate the West Tisbury 5, the women who traveled to Williamston, North Carolina, in 1964. It is situated in front of the old West Tisbury Library on Music Street. A complementary plaque was placed at St. Andrew's Episcopal Church on North Summer Street in Edgartown to acknowledge the re-formation of the NAACP chapter on the Vineyard. It also recognizes the five West Tisbury women for "placing personal safety at risk, they traveled to the South to register voters." (The dates on the plaques in Edgartown and West Tisbury should be reversed.)

At the 2008 ceremony in Edgartown, three people present were teenage members of the NAACP in 1963: Dianne Powers, Tony Alleyne and Bob Tankard. Other participants included Nancy Smith, Audrey LeVasseur, Chris Murphy, Polly Murphy, Woollcott Smith and Peg Lilienthal. And a number of now deceased people were recognized: Reverend Henry Bird, George Jacobs, Nancy Whiting, Audria Tankard, Kivi Kaplan and Toby and Lucille Dorsey.

The Heritage Trail received another grant, this time for $2,000, from the Massachusetts Foundation of Humanities in 2007. The trail has been

Like the Martin house on Chappaquiddick, the Gospel Tabernacle is sadly in need of repair. It flourished in the 1950s, when the Reverends Charles and Scotta Johnson ministered to a summer congregation. *Photo by Joyce Dresser.*

hailed by the *Cape Cod Times*, the *Boston Globe* and even the *New York Times*, which sent a reporter and photographer to the dedication ceremony of the Dorothy West house in 2008.

Two more sites were dedicated in February 2010. At the high school, a plaque was placed in honor of Quinton Bannister, the first African American teacher at the school. Mr. Bannister retired after thirty-two years of teaching history and law. A second plaque was placed in Vineyard Haven in honor of William Hammond, who operated his barbershop there for forty years.

A new edition of *Lighting the Trail* is scheduled for publication and is again supported by the Massachusetts Foundation for the Humanities; it includes new sites and updates on current material. It is impressive that this project continues to generate interest, expand its findings and promote the trail, both within the school system and in the community at large. Dr. Weintraub and Carrie Tankard are to be commended for their efforts.

Adam Clayton Powell Jr. (1908–1972) purchased this house in 1937 with his wife, but they divorced in 1945, the year he was elected to Congress. He served until 1970. Powell organized strikes, pickets and boycotts in the 1930s on behalf of African Americans in New York City. Isabel (1909–2008) was a nightclub entertainer and a special education teacher in New York for thirty years. She maintained her summer residence in the Highlands, enjoying popularity as the grande dame, Bloody Mary in hand. *Photo by Joyce Dresser.*

***

Nearly two dozen sites define the African American Heritage Trail of Martha's Vineyard as of 2010. Many sites earned positive press coverage at their dedication ceremonies. Visitors are encouraged to arrange a tour of the African American Heritage Trail, to buy the book *Lighting the Trail* and to support the efforts of the trail. It is costly to create new sites along the trail. Income is generated primarily through book sales, grants and personal contributions.

As noted on the website, the trail has defined its mission as, "To continue to research and publish previously undocumented history and to involve the Island community in the identification and celebration of the contributions made by people of color to the island of Martha's Vineyard."

Heritage Trail

Because the African American Heritage Trail of Martha's Vineyard has been included in the curriculum for sophomores at the regional high school, students now have a broader view of the Vineyard's varied heritage. Each year, sophomores board buses and journey around the Island on a tour of many of the key sites along the trail. This program has added to the depth and perspective that students achieve in their understanding of the breadth of Martha's Vineyard's history.

Following is a list of sites on the African American Heritage Trail of Martha's Vineyard. The sites are listed in the chronological order that a plaque was affixed to the structure to commemorate that a significant person, place or event occurred that was memorable to the African American community. For more background on the individual sites, check the website mvheritagetrail.org or consult the book *Lighting the Trail*, which expounds in detail on the individual sites along the route.

1. Shearer Cottage—Morgan Avenue, in the Highlands, by the Baptist Temple, Oak Bluffs: August 1997
2. Eastville Cemetery—adjacent to the Lobster Hatchery, in Oak Bluffs: June 1998
3. Nancy Michael—Memorial Wharf, Edgartown: October 1998
4. MVRHS—Jannifer Chronicles and high school teams: June 1999
5. Pulpit Rock—off County Road, in Oak Bluffs: October 1999
6. Landladies Cottages and memorial bench—lower Circuit Avenue, Oak Bluffs: October 2000
7. Randall Burton—Menemsha, Chilmark and West Basin, Aquinnah sites: August 2001
8. Rebecca Amos—Great Rock Bight, North Road, Chilmark: 2002
9. Powell Cottage—Dorothy West Avenue in the Highlands, Oak Bluffs: August 2003
10. Grace Church—Bishop Burgess in Vineyard Haven: September 2003
11. Brooke House—on Nashawena Avenue, Oak Bluffs: October 2003
12. Overton House—on Narragansett Avenue, Oak Bluffs: September 2004
13. Cottagers Corner—on Pequot Avenue, Oak Bluffs: July 2006
14. West Tisbury 5—Music Street, at old West Tisbury library: September 2007
15. NAACP re-formed—St. Andrew's, Winter Street, Edgartown: January 2008
16. Island educators—Manning, Shorter, Tankard, Tisbury: May 2008
17. Dorothy West House—Myrtle Avenue, in the Highlands, Oak Bluffs: August 2008

18. Barber Hammond—Main Street, Vineyard Haven: February 2010
19. Quinton Bannister—high school teacher, MVRHS: February 2010
William Martin House—on Chappaquiddick
Grave of Martin—on Chappaquiddick
Bradley Church—Masonic Avenue, Oak Bluffs
Gospel Tabernacle Pentecostal Church—on Dukes County Avenue, Oak Bluffs

One-hour tours can be arranged to view the Oak Bluffs sites, or longer tours can be taken around the Island. The African American Heritage Trail of Martha's Vineyard is a vibrant reminder of the impact of African Americans.

Chapter 11

MR. PRESIDENT

In the late summer of 2004, Barack Obama, a candidate for the United States Senate from Illinois, agreed to participate in a forum on race relations held at the Old Whaling Church in Edgartown, moderated by his former Harvard professor, Charles Ogletree. The forum is held annually on the Vineyard to promote a deeper understanding of the relations that have evolved between the races. This year, the enticement was Mr. Obama, who had just delivered the ringing keynote speech at the Democratic National Convention in Boston the month before.

"Charismatic new voice of the Democratic party," gushed C.K. Wolfson in her *Gazette* review of Mr. Obama's comments to a full hall. Obama began with the theme he used to endorse John Kerry's candidacy for president, using his background as a child of an African father and a white woman from Kansas, born in Hawaii—the point being, anyone can enter politics.

Obama presented himself in a casual demeanor but made his key points with emphasis, observing that it was the need to achieve a political majority that had motivated him to enter politics to get things done. It was a rousing speech, and even then, Obama had a clear grasp of the importance of seeing the global view of race relations when he said, "If we deal with race in isolation, to the exclusion of jobs or the health crisis, we'll lose. We need to break out of the either/or mentality." He closed with the words of Reverend Martin Luther King Jr.: "Although the arc of the human universe is long, it bends toward justice, but it doesn't bend by itself." The crowd gave him a standing ovation.

Other participants in the forum offered insight and advice on how to advance the cause of racial equity. Professor Caroline Huxby advocated a goal to excel in science and math, and Dr. Abigail Thernstram suggested that schools must be more proactive. Grass-roots mobilization was advanced by Professor Sheryll Cashin. Professor Lani Guinier noted that the right to vote is determined by individual states and then echoed Obama's comments when she said, "Race is a means for masking class. We use the language of race to avoid what's happening. We need to learn to talk about race and class in the same sentence, or we will be here fifty years from now talking about the same questions." More than once the issue of class distinction arose in the discussion of race relations. And just as the issue has to be considered as part of the whole political landscape, the impact of class distinctions figures prominently in a discussion of race relations.

The crowd was energized, enthusiastic and invigorated. So, apparently, was Barack Obama, because he returned to the Vineyard in the summer of 2007 as he was laying the groundwork for his run for the presidency. And one Vineyarder kept a close eye on the future president.

***

Over three days in the summer of 2007, when Barack Obama was an Illinois senator running for president, George Gamble of Oak Bluffs (former owner of Among the Flowers Café in Edgartown) ran into the future president. Three times.

On his way home from the beach one sunny afternoon—it was August 29, to be exact—George noticed several secret service people gathered at Donny Gregory's bike shop in downtown Oak Bluffs. He suspected they were secret service agents because they wore earpieces. George and his daughter-in-law Kathleen walked into the rental area and heard that Senator Obama was renting bicycles, not just for his family, but for his entire secret service contingent.

When the senator offered his credit card, George overheard Mr. Gregory say, "This one's on me. This is my contribution to your campaign." Barack's answer was, "No, you're a hardworking man, and I cannot accept your offer." After a few more exchanges, Mr. Gregory accepted his credit card. As Barack turned to leave with his bike, George approached him, shook his hand and wished him well in his bid for the presidency. George was impressed with his firm handshake.

The next day, George was in Edgartown at the stop sign at the corner of Main Street and the Edgartown West Tisbury Road. An "army" of bikers approached, headed into downtown Edgartown, with Barack Obama in the lead. George recognized him immediately, leaned out of his window and greeted him for the second day with a "Hello, Senator." Barack Obama replied with a friendly "Hello."

On day three, Friday, August 31, 2007, George had lunch at Farm Neck Country Club. As he was leaving the dining room, Barack Obama and Vernon Jordon were entering. George held the door for the two men and greeted the senator for the third time in three days. At this point, George began to wonder if Senator Obama recognized him or if Obama might think he was being stalked. Yet these were purely chance encounters.

George recounted his three exchanges with Senator Obama to a neighbor, who was duly impressed by the sightings. She, too, had seen Senator and Michelle Obama. She approached the secret service to ask if they would get Michelle's attention so she could say hello. "Why?" they wanted to know. She explained that she and Michelle had gone to Princeton at the same time and knew each other quite well, in the small contingent of African American students. Unfortunately, the secret service either did not believe the neighbor or did not think it warranted disturbing Michelle.

That August proved a busy time for presidential hopefuls on the Vineyard. Barack Obama held a fundraiser, as did Hillary Clinton, John Edwards and Mitt Romney. There is a lot of summer money on the Vineyard, and presidential candidates want a portion of the pie.

Barack Obama won the presidential election on November 4, 2008, by a margin of 52 percent to 45 percent, claiming 365 electoral votes to John McCain's 173. By and large, Obama won the East and West Coasts, and McCain won the heartland and much of the South. It was the first election between two sitting senators. It was the first time a Catholic had been elected vice president. It was the first time in half a century that an incumbent was not a candidate. And, of course, it was the first time an African American had ever been elected president of the United States.

On Martha's Vineyard, Barack Obama secured 75 percent of the total vote, enticing an amazing 82 percent of the 12,845 registered voters to the polls. The most solidly Democratic town in the commonwealth of Massachusetts was Aquinnah, which showered Mr. Obama with 90 percent of its votes. In descending order, West Tisbury voted 84 percent for Obama, Chilmark 83 percent, Tisbury 77 percent, Oak Bluffs 73 percent, Edgartown 70 percent and Gosnold, the island of Cuttyhunk, gave him 66 percent. Overall, the Vineyard stood solidly behind the new president.

***

Rumors flew across the wire services and the Internet in the early summer of 2009. The tease was that the first family intended to take a Vineyard vacation. Excitement reached a fever pitch. Whether it was the lure of the land from his previous visits, following in President Clinton's footsteps, the search for an idyllic island getaway or the appeal of an African American enclave replete with Harvard professors, prominent people and a trio of golf courses, the Obamas chose Martha's Vineyard for their first family vacation as the First Family.

Martha's Vineyard Magazine put Obama and the Clintons on its cover. Michael West observed, "The Vineyard Obameter indicates the aura about the new president is still aglow. If the first family does vacation on the Vineyard this summer, as has been reported, the heat will only increase."

The site the family rented, for a reputed $40,000 a week, was the Blue Heron Farm on the Chilmark West Tisbury town line, a twenty-eight-acre estate with a pristine Victorian farmhouse, hay barn, shed, tennis and basketball courts, golf tee, gardens, orchard and a modicum of presidential privacy. The property had been purchased in 2005 for $20 million by William and Mollie Van Devender; it was a quality hideaway. And the element of security was key; the site is removed from the excitement of the down-Island community but accessible to prime (golf) sites, should the need arise.

Besides security on the ground, there was security in the air. Federal planes and helicopters preempted airspace during the presidential visit, scheduled for August 23 to 30, 2009. A month before the president's arrival, local pilots worried about restricted airspace around the Vineyard. Satellite towers poked through the trees to ensure proper communications; the Oak Bluffs school, in summer recess, served as the center for public pronouncements.

Before the president's plane touched down, another contingent, besides the secret service, prepared for the visit. "The Obamas are vacationing on Martha's Vineyard, and the only ones working harder than the Secret Service agents to get ready are the souvenir shop, restaurant and other store owners, scrambling to stock and sell T-shirts, posters and muffins commemorating the Obamas' first vacation as first family."[61] Special commercial ventures ranged from Off-shore Ale's Ale to the Chief to a Bobama T-shirt from Good Dog Goods. The Vineyard's Chamber of Commerce executive director was giddy with excitement: "I think President Obama represents so much that people are excited about," said Nancy Gardella. And Roger Schilling of C'est La Vie, an eclectic boutique, was quoted as saying, "People, rich and poor, black and white, are smiling."

The Obamas arrived in a hurricane and left in a storm; it was quite a week. Hurricane Bill—the storm, not the former president—hovered off the Maine coast as Air Force One landed at the Cape Cod Coast Guard Station. The Obamas were transported to the Martha's Vineyard Airport by helicopter on Sunday afternoon, August 23, 2009. A number of hardy locals lined the street waving and cheering the president's arrival; one welcoming sign read, "Obama, take a deep breath and relax."

On Monday, that was the intent. At the communication headquarters, the deputy press secretary announced, "The president is taking it easy." He played tennis with Michelle and a round of golf at Farm Neck and dined with advisor Valerie Jarrett. That was likely the most relaxation the president enjoyed all week.

On Tuesday, August 25, Obama ventured off to Mink Meadows in Tisbury and played nine holes of golf. One wonk noted that the presidential visit preempted the "Public Welcome" sign that hangs at the Mink Meadows course, but no one was worried about losing tee time so the president could play through.

At lunch on Tuesday, Obama was spotted at Nancy's Restaurant in downtown Oak Bluffs, and his order of fried shrimp, calamari, scallops and French fries was posted on Facebook before he could sit down to enjoy the repast at the home of Valerie Jarrett on East Chop.

Once again, serendipitous cyclist George Gamble was on the scene. He heard the rumor that President Obama's motorcade was heading to East Chop. Curious, George hopped on his bike and, using knowledge of the back roads, found the home where the president had gone with his party. The secret service kept George at a safe distance, and he struck up a conversation with other onlookers. Although he didn't actually see the president, he considers this his fourth Obama encounter.

That evening, the excitement focused on several restaurants along Circuit Avenue in Oak Bluffs. Hundreds of onlookers gawked as the motorcade eventually approached downtown. The Obamas settled on Sweet Life Cafe, which no doubt pleased owner Pierre Guerin. For the rest of the summer, he happily pointed out which table the Obamas had dined at.

All the hoopla brought an admonition from the *Vineyard Gazette* to allow the president some breathing room. "Visitors, from presidents to kings to ordinary folk, come to the Island for a change in the pace of life. They come for the quiet, the privacy and the beauty of this fragile place in the sea. They come because the Vineyard offers a slower pace of life."

And yet, there was work to be done. The *Boston Herald*, not exactly an Obama sycophant, announced, "President Obama interrupted his

Martha's Vineyard vacation to reappoint Ben Bernanke for a second term as head of the Federal Reserve, despite some grumbling that Bernanke's past monetary policies were partly to blame for the financial mess that's engulfed the nation."

And there were protests planned, on land and at sea. "Noted war protester Cindy Sheehan is scheduled to arrive today on Martha's Vineyard to hold a series of peace vigils and other events to confront the President about the continuing wars in Iraq and Afghanistan."[62] And a flotilla of five fishing boats steamed over from New Bedford to Vineyard Haven to protest changes in federal fishing regulations. Both protests were peaceful, under the watchful eyes of the secret service, but their presence preempted the relaxing atmosphere the Vineyard hoped to grant the president.

Wednesday morning at 2:00 a.m., the president was awakened and informed that Senator Ted Kennedy had passed away Tuesday night. The weather precluded any attempt at golf or a public outing that day, and the First Family stayed close to home.

By Thursday, August 27, the sun was out. The press was unsure what was happening, and after a number of false starts, the Obamas were spotted

Everybody wants to visit the Gay Head Lighthouse at the tip of the Vineyard. *Left to right*: President Obama, Sasha, Joan LeLacheur (wife of lighthouse keeper Richard Skidmore), Michelle Obama and Malia. *Courtesy of Tom Wallace, Wallace & Co. Sotheby's International Realty.*

biking in Aquinnah. The president committed his most grievous faux pas of the week by being photographed sans bike helmet. The First Family toured the Gay Head lighthouse and agreed to be photographed with the lighthouse keeper's wife. President Obama managed to squeeze in another round of golf, this time at the Vineyard Golf Club. It was noted in the *New York Times* that the president was casual in his game, and his aides were reluctant to reveal his scores.

Again, the *Gazette* offered a word of caution: "Presidents deserve some quality time away from the pressure of the office and it is to be hoped the Vineyard offers at least a few true vacation interludes between interruptions."

President and Mrs. Obama flew to Boston Friday evening, August 28, to avoid Hurricane Danny and prepare for the funeral of Senator Kennedy. Obama delivered a ringing eulogy at the packed service Saturday morning, then returned to the Vineyard Saturday afternoon. (Malia and Sasha remained on the Vineyard over the weekend.)

And then it was Sunday, August 30, and the vacation was all but over. With niece Suhalia Ng and Sasha and Malia, Barack Obama made a quick trip to Alley's General Store and Garcia's to stock up on candy, gum and oatmeal cookies. They boarded the helicopter and lifted off from the Martha's Vineyard Airport at 4:23 p.m., Sunday afternoon, August 30. It had been a whirlwind week for the first African American president, and he left the Vineyard impressed, energized and exhausted by the constant stream of activity and attention.

In 2010, the Vineyard was flattered that President Obama returned to savor the tranquility of our peaceful Island.

Chapter 12

PROMINENT PEOPLE

Many prominent African Americans have called the Vineyard home, or summer home, or expressed a fond appreciation for the charm and character of Martha's Vineyard. Many people have left a lasting impression on the community during their tenure on Island. As generations age, it is important to treasure the impact of our forebears, to recognize the prominent people in our midst, to savor the moment of our time on this little piece of paradise, even as we make room for the next generation. Within the African American community are layers and levels of influence that we want to recognize, acknowledge and preserve as we move forward.

The following names are by no means exclusive or extensive. They serve only to recognize a few of the well-known artists and writers, performers and producers, movers and shakers who consider Martha's Vineyard a signal part of their lives. As Diane Jones said recently, "I'm already planning my Vineyard vacation. That's what keeps me going through the long winter." For her to say how eagerly she anticipates her time on the Vineyard, we know we live in a very special place. From kings to presidents to ordinary people, Martha's Vineyard offers a salvation, a respite, a break from the pressures of modern life, a chance to sit back, relax and appreciate who we are, where we have been and where we are going.

***

Marla Blakey was born in Washington, D.C., and grew up in Roxbury, Massachusetts, but came to the Vineyard as a teenager for summer family vacations in the 1960s, as many African Americans did. Her father, Ruble Blakey, sang jazz with Lionel Hampton. Her mother built a house on the Vineyard, which Marla calls home, so her ties to the Island are deep, though her time on the Vineyard has been more fleeting in her adult life.

At the age of seventeen, Marla worked as a dancer/show girl in an all-black revue in Atlantic City, New Jersey, at the Club Harlem, second only to the Cotton Club in New York. "I started out at the top," she says, working with the likes of Duke Ellington, Cab Calloway, Moms Mabley, Billy Eckstein and Sammy Davis Jr. Imagine that roster of co-workers in your first professional job! "It was an amazing introduction to show business," she says. And it made her grow up fast, working with consummate professionals, learning the ethics and respect for show business.

One sour note occurred when Marla Blakey was in a show entitled *Sepia Revue*, which opened in Las Vegas in 1969. It was an all-black show and proved very successful, but resentment arose at its success. One night after a performance, police entered the dressing room, handcuffed the performers and jailed them for failure to purchase a work permit, at a cost of $3.50 per card. That incident and verbal harassment on the Strip because they were black, were unpleasant memories Marla harbors from the sixties. She admits, however, that the incident she incurred was minor compared to the horrors and hardships others endured during those times.

From the success of Club Harlem, Marla danced at army bases in Europe, then organized her own dance troupe and dance studio in Boston before she moved on to Hollywood. A big break occurred when she ran into a high school classmate, Donna Summer, who offered her a job. "I was lucky," Marla admits. She spent the early 1980s in Los Angeles staging and choreographing shows and music videos for performers such as ZZ Top, David Bowie, Linda Ronstadt, Aretha Franklin, Sting, Fleetwood Mac and several Motown groups. Music videos were then at their height of popularity.

But the music business slowed down in the mid-1980s. Marla longed for New England friends and family. She left Los Angeles for the Vineyard in 1988 to be close to her mother and their summer home, and she has been here ever since. She staged her first big production on the Vineyard, *For Colored Girls Who Have Considered Suicide When the Rainbow Is Enuf*, at the Whaling Church in Edgartown with sixteen sold-out performances in 1989. Marla Blakey has since directed plays at the Vineyard Playhouse, produced Jazz Fests at Featherstone and even did a stint as a DJ at a local club.

She says, "You're only as good as your last job," and that mantra keeps her performing in a professional manner, with high standards. She is eternally grateful for the enduring support of the local Vineyard community and especially her dear friends on the Vineyard. Marla does regret how difficult it is for some young people of black families who can't afford or don't feel the need to maintain their family's home. She fears the loss of history, the fading of the heritage of those brave and hardy African Americans who struggled to get a foothold on the Island, like her mother. She hopes that they, and she, will be able to honor those who came before.

Senator Edward W. Brooke was born in Washington, D.C., in 1919 and graduated from Howard University. During World War II, he served as an officer in the segregated 366th Infantry Regiment, initially stationed at Fort Devens. It was from there that he first visited the Vineyard in the 1940s. During the war, Brooke was involved in the European theatre, specifically in Italy.

Brooke enrolled at Boston University law school and graduated in 1948. Ten years later, he purchased a pair of houses on Nashawena Park in Oak Bluffs, just up from the Inkwell. He sought to develop a social club for African Americans but met with resistance, and the plan was dropped. This became his vacation retreat as he entered the political arena.

In his first successful statewide election, he earned the confidence of voters to serve as the first African American state attorney general in the country. During four years in office (1963–67), he cultivated a reputation for targeting organized crime and prosecuted the Boston Strangler.

Edward Brooke used his position as attorney general as a springboard to launch his campaign to become the first African American elected to the United States Senate by popular vote, a position he served admirably from 1967 to 1979. During his two terms, he was a strong advocate of a woman's right to choose, epitomized by the *Roe v. Wade* Supreme Court decision in 1973, and worked diligently on the equal employment opportunity act, voting rights and education reform. He was the first Republican senator to call for Richard Nixon to resign following the Watergate scandal.

As noted, the Edward W. Brooke Courthouse was renamed in his honor in 2000. Three years later, his home was recognized as a site on the African American Heritage Trail. (He actually sold the house to his sister and niece in 1977.) In 2004, Senator Brooke was awarded the Presidential Medal of Freedom. A book signing for his autobiography, *Bridging the Divide: My Life*, drew throngs of old friends and supporters to the Oak Bluffs Library in 2006. In October 2009, Senator Brooke was awarded the Congressional Gold Medal.

Senator Edward W. Brooke, born in Washington, D.C., in 1919, graduated from Howard University and served in combat during World War II. He was the first African American elected to the United States Senate by popular vote and served from 1967 to 1979. This was his summer home. *Photo by Joyce Dresser.*

Adelaide Cromwell, like her cousin Senator Brooke, was born in 1919 in Washington, D.C. While Senator Brooke was the politician, Adelaide Cromwell has epitomized the academic. She graduated from Smith College and earned a master's at the University of Pennsylvania during World War II, when she first visited the Vineyard. She said recently that she still considers the Vineyard her second home and plans to come down in the warmer weather. She has summered on the Island since 1943.

In 1946, Dr. Cromwell earned her doctorate in sociology from Radcliffe College, now part of Harvard. She taught at both Hunter College and her alma mater, Smith. Dr. Cromwell was hired as a professor of sociology at Boston University in 1951 and served in that capacity until her retirement in 1985, more than thirty years. At the onset of her tenure, she was instrumental in establishing the African Studies Program and later was appointed director of the graduate program in Afro-American Studies.

Adelaide Cromwell dedicated her career to education, research and writing, which benefited both her students and herself. She contributed an essay to the *Dukes County Intelligencer* in 1984 entitled "The History of Oak Bluffs as a Popular Resort for Blacks." The subtitle of this groundbreaking piece was "From Servants to Celebrities All Enjoyed the Pleasures of the Vineyard." Her books include *The Other Brahmins, Boston's Black Upper Class: 1750–1950* (1994) and *Unveiled Voices Unvarnished Memories, The Cromwell Family in Slavery and Segregation, 1992–1972* (2007).

Dr. Cromwell has a host of Vineyard friends and connections as a result of nearly seventy years of Vineyard visits. She is a strong advocate of the history of the African American community on the Vineyard. Her influence is felt from the heritage of the Shearer Cottage to historian Robert Hayden, and with her longtime friend Betty Rawlins. She is a woman held in high esteem.

Henry Louis "Skip" Gates, born in 1950, is a professor at Harvard who vacations regularly on Martha's Vineyard. He is a literary critic and a public intellectual with an array of awards for his research on African American heritage and culture. His 2003 book, *The Trials of Phillis Wheatley*, evolved from his research on the published works of the first African American female poet, enslaved in 1761 by a Boston family at the age of eight. Professor Gates had a PBS series on the genealogy of prominent African Americans. He is the director of the W.E.B. Du Bois Institute for African and African American Research at Harvard and is a leading African American scholar.

His arrest in his Cambridge home in July 2009 sparked outrage from all quarters on racial profiling and the interaction between police and homeowners. When President Obama opined on the matter, the issue begged resolution and was settled, to a degree, in the infamous "beer summit" at the White House. According to Professor Gates, it turns out that he and Sergeant Crowley, the arresting officer, are both distantly related to Confederate general Nathan Bedford Forrest.

Professor Gates visits the Vineyard regularly, renting different sites and often riding his red tricycle along the bicycle path on Beach Road. Due to a childhood football injury, one leg is shorter than the other, so a bicycle or a cane can ease his mobility. On Island, he maintains a disciplined routine, appreciating the atmosphere of a vacation site but making his writing and research a prominent part of each day. As the author of nearly a dozen books, and myriad articles, Skip Gates is the consummate professor.

Professor Gates is impressed by the number of upper- and middle-class African Americans who live or vacation on the Vineyard, making it a hospitable environment for African American and mixed-race children to mingle with peers. He enjoys the Vineyard, from the stimulating environment to the social setting of intellectual leaders.

Della Hardman (1922–2005) was raised in West Virginia and graduated from West Virginia State College in 1943, studied at the Massachusetts College of Art and earned her master's degree from Boston University in 1945. In 1994, at the age of seventy-two, Della Hardman was granted her doctorate from Kent State University in Ohio.

Born the granddaughter of slaves, she sought a career in art. Much of her life was spent as an artist who taught college, as well as a poet. Dr. Hardman first visited the Vineyard in the 1930s but only moved to the Island after her retirement from teaching in 1986. The following year, she married her childhood sweetheart, Leon Hardman, and settled into the Vineyard community.

She succeeded Dorothy West as the Oak Bluffs columnist for the *Vineyard Gazette*. In fact, she was so dedicated to the responsibilities incumbent on writing the weekly column that she refused to be admitted to the hospital until she had filed her piece, on deadline. Henry Louis Gates, a fellow West Virginian, was quoted at her death: "She brought a renewed vitality to the African-American community on the Vineyard, and the community brought renewed vigor to her life."

One of her favorite sayings, a phrase that lingers on during Oak Bluffs's annual Della Hardman Day, is a poignant reflection on her life: "Savor the moment."

Charlayne Hunter-Gault was encouraged by African American businessmen and civic leaders to apply to the University of Georgia, then a segregated university. Her admission was eventually accepted; she was admitted in 1961, survived initial insults and harassment and graduated in 1963. A hall was named for her and fellow African American Hamilton Holmes at the University of Georgia in 2001, the fortieth anniversary of the desegregation of the school.

Ms. Hunter-Gault pursued a career in journalism as the first African American female contributor to the *New Yorker*, then with the PBS McNeil-Lehrer Newshour as national correspondent and substitute anchor from 1978 to 1997. In 1999 she switched to CNN, where she was South African bureau chief. Her autobiography, *In My Place*, recounts her African American experience in the 1950s at the inception of the civil rights movement. Her research on Africa resulted in *New News out of Africa: Uncovering Africa's Renaissance.*

Hunter-Gault made her first visit to the Vineyard in 1970 with her husband, investment banker Ron Gault. Each summer they returned for vacation until they bought a house in Oak Bluffs. Now she commutes between homes in Johannesburg, South Africa, and Oak Bluffs. Hunter-Gault immerses herself in the Vineyard atmosphere, from tennis to socializing to yard sale scavenging. In an interview, Hunter-Gault compared the Vineyard to her childhood home in Georgia: "There are few places with a strong sense of community,"[63] she says. "The Vineyard is like a small town even when it swells to 100,000. Although I meet new people all the time, I have a coterie of friends that is a constant in my life. Sometimes we just have fun, like sit on the porch, look at the sea, and watch motorcycles ride by." She has captured the vacation atmosphere of the Vineyard.

Lois Mailou Jones (1905–1998) was born in Boston. She became intrigued with art at an early age, during summers spent on Martha's Vineyard. She once said, "Every summer of my childhood, my mother took me and my brother to Martha's Vineyard Island. I began painting in watercolor, my pet medium." She appreciated the beauty of the Vineyard landscape.

After high school, Jones was one of two African American students invited to study at the Museum of Fine Arts in Boston; but when she sought to teach there, she was referred elsewhere. Ms. Jones grew interested in textile design. In 1930, she was hired as a professor of art at Howard University in Washington, D.C., where she taught until 1977, nearly half a century. She earned her degree from Howard in 1945.

As an artist in the era of the Harlem Renaissance, she was recognized as a mentor as well as a fine artist in her own right. Jones's 1932 painting, *The Ascent of Ethiopia*, unites African heritage with the Harlem Renaissance in an expression of the struggles endured by African Americans to gain a foothold in America.

Jones was unaccustomed to the blatant racism she encountered in Washington but refused to let it deter her from her teaching or her art. A year in Paris, freed from racial bigotry, allowed her to paint *Les Fetiches*, which combined African tradition with Western culture, using African masks. The piece now hangs at the Smithsonian and is considered one of her best-known works.

Returning home, race reared its ugly head. At a Washington gallery, she had to enter a competition using a white friend's name; her painting, *Indian Shops, Gay Head*, won top prize.

In 1953, Jones married a Haitian artist and felt the influence of the Haitian culture, with an African heritage. In 1963, she created *Challenge America*, a collage commemorating the March on Washington.

In 1973, Jones became the first African American artist with a solo show at the Boston Museum of Fine Arts. Bill and Hillary Clinton purchased her Vineyard seascape, *Breezy Day at Gay Head*.

All her life, Lois Mailou Jones struggled to prove that she was an artist, first. Her niece, Jacqueline Holland, wrote, "Lois describes herself, quite rightly, as an American artist who happened to be black."[64] At her death, in 1998, Jones was considered the longest-surviving artist of the Harlem Renaissance. She is buried in Oak Bluffs.

Spike Lee has a house in Oak Bluffs and frequently visits the Vineyard. Over the past quarter century, through his film company, 40 Acres and a Mule Filmworks, he has produced more than three dozen movies. Many of his films focus on the impact of the media, race relations, poverty and urban crises, as well as political issues of the day. Topical films include *Malcolm X*, the Birmingham church bombing in 1963 and his 2006 TV documentary *When the Levees Broke: A Requiem in Four Acts*, delving into hurricane-ravaged New Orleans after Katrina. Spike Lee has directed numerous television commercials, including one with a car driving off the Martha's Vineyard ferry. His vendors include Nike's Air Jordan, Taco Bell and Ben & Jerry's.

Jill Nelson grew up in Harlem and still calls it home, though she has summered on the Vineyard all her life. She graduated from Columbia School of Journalism and has made writing her career. Articles with her byline have been published in the *New York Times*, *Essence* and the *Village Voice*, among other publications. Her memoir, *Volunteer Slavery: My Authentic Negro Experience*, explores her involvement as a black female journalist with the *Washington Post*; it won an American Book Award. She has written half a dozen books, but the most relevant Vineyard book is *Finding Martha's Vineyard, African Americans at Home on an Island*, (2005) part memoir, part history, with brief biographies of prominent acquaintances and a few recipes thrown in. It's a charming account of the appreciation and admiration Jill feels for the Vineyard.

Professor Charles Ogletree has summered on the Vineyard since 1995. This eminent professor taught both Michelle and Barack Obama at Harvard Law School. As an attorney, Charles Ogletree has proven himself to be a forceful advocate of the right for a fair trial, especially as it relates to African Americans. Professor Ogletree is a frequent moderator and author of opinion pieces on civil rights and has written half a dozen books on such topics as segregation in education, the rights of the accused and the Supreme Court. Robert Hayden profiled Professor Ogletree in his well-researched book, *African Americans on Martha's Vineyard*: "His forum leadership and participation in conceptualizing, interpreting and coordinating public events on Martha's Vineyard is noteworthy and typical of the role he plays on a national level on legal-social and political equity issues in America."

And Professor Ogletree is an avid fisherman. "He goes out thirty to thirty-five times a season," says charter boat captain Buddy Vanderhoop of Aquinnah. "He blocks out fishing time and brings former classmates or other professors. He's an unbelievable fisherman." The professor prefers striped bass and bluefish but is also partial to tuna, confides Mr. Vanderhoop. "And he knows people from all over. You never know who he'll bring along. He's a great guy." And when Buddy is busy, Gordon Thompson, Mabelle and Sam's son, is more than willing to help out.

As Mr. Hayden notes, "Martha's Vineyard is fortunate to have him on the Island."

Vera and Rufus Shorter moved to the Vineyard in 1976 when Rufus was appointed superintendent of the Martha's Vineyard schools, the first African American in that position. (Kriner Cash was the second.) The Shorters had been frequent Vineyard vacationers, but when the former teacher and administrator was hired for the top job, they committed to enjoy the Vineyard lifestyle year-round.

Rufus Shorter was instrumental in coordinating efforts across the Island to construct the Performing Arts Center (PAC) at the high school. During his abbreviated tenure (he died in 1980 after only four years in the position), he worked tirelessly with the school committee to approve additional classroom space for culinary arts, automotive instruction and the performing arts. The PAC was nearly complete when he passed away. Mrs. Shorter stated of her husband, "He made a major contribution to the arts on the Vineyard with the PAC."

During the 1960s, Vera Shorter was an activist in Brooklyn, serving as an advisor to the citywide youth project, picketing banks that refused to employ blacks as tellers or custodians and protesting skating rinks that denied access to blacks because they were not members, then restricting membership.

Of the African American experience on the Vineyard, Mrs. Shorter was impressed by the efforts in the late 1890s of Susan Bradley, who worked with

Portuguese immigrants at what became the Bradley Mission. "They were the lower echelon on the Vineyard; the Wasps and Brahmins ran things. She included everyone in her mission. She always struck me as being so generous, ahead of her time."

Mrs. Shorter earned the Living Legend Award from the NAACP. "Actually," she said, "it's for an accumulation of work for the NAACP and community action." Over the years, she has served on the board of the Nathan Mayhew Seminars, Community Services and the Martha's Vineyard Hospital. At eighty-seven, she shows no signs of slowing down. "The award," she smiles, "is for my alleged good works."

Mrs. Shorter is charged with seeking legal redress for employment and housing issues by the local NAACP. Her cases are confidential, yet she confirmed a pattern of racism that is different, in a way, from "conventional" racism. Middle-class African Americans are treated fairly, but poor blacks, Brazilians and poor whites are discriminated against. "It's a war against the poor," she said. "It's subtle, but it's there." It appears to be more an issue of class than racial distinction. She acknowledged that there is less contempt for poor people on the Vineyard than in the urban center, but it is evident—indeed, prevalent—among the blue-collar crowd. In her role of legal redress, she handles cases in the school system and employment issues. Sometimes, she said, white people do not think before they speak; their cruel comments are unconscious.

She is pleased that the NAACP has an advisory role on the school curriculum and is invited to sit in on the selection process for hiring new educators. She is a supporter of the Heritage Trail as part of the high school curriculum. "I don't know anyone who's against that," she said. And she was very impressed with the articulation and awareness exhibited by the students about the role of the trail in recognizing African Americans on Martha's Vineyard.

Dorothy West (1907–1998) was born in Boston and moved to Harlem in 1926 with her cousin, the poet Helene Johnson. In New York, West became acquainted with luminaries in the literary world that evolved into the Harlem Renaissance, including Langston Hughes, Countee Cullen and the novelist Wallace Thurman. It was Langston Hughes who nicknamed West "the Kid" because of her youth; she was only nineteen. "We didn't know it was the Harlem Renaissance, because we were all young and all poor," Miss West was quoted as saying by the Associated Press in 1995. "We had no jobs to speak of, and we had rent parties to raise rent money."

When the Dorothy West (1907–1998) house was dedicated as a site on the African American Heritage Trail in 2008, the story was covered by the *New York Times*. *Photo by Joyce Dresser.*

In 1934, Dorothy West edited the magazine *Challenge*, with its successor, *New Challenge*, dedicated to the publication of African American literature. *Challenge* printed essays by Ralph Ellison, Margaret Walker and Richard Wright. Later, West worked on the Federal Writers' Project, a program in the Works Progress Administration of the New Deal.

When she moved to the Vineyard in 1948, she wrote an autobiographical novel, *The Living Is Easy*, a satirical tale about Boston's black middle class and family dynamics. The introduction was written by her friend Adelaide Cromwell. When the book was republished in 1982, it was considered a requisite text in female African American literature.

Jacqueline Kennedy Onassis was an editor for Doubleday, the intended publisher for Dorothy West's second novel. An apocryphal story recounted that Jackie drove twenty miles from her summer home in Aquinnah to meet Dorothy in her little house in Oak Bluffs to review the final galleys of *The Wedding*. When Jackie entered Dorothy's tiny domicile, she looked around. Every chair and couch was covered with piles of papers, books, manuscripts and other literary ephemera. Jackie asked Dorothy, "Where shall we sit?" Dorothy shrugged and said, "Right here," motioning to the floor. So the former first lady and "the Kid" got to work on the living room rug.

At the age of eighty-eight, in 1995, Dorothy West finished *The Wedding* and dedicated it to her editor, Jackie Kennedy Onassis, who had passed away the year before. *The Wedding* is set in the Oval, a takeoff on the Highlands in East Chop, populated by upper-class black professionals. The theme is that the daughter of a prominent African American family, the Coles, a beauty who could have any man on her dance card, chooses to wed a white musician, sending seismic waves through five generations of this African American bourgeoisie community. "An intimate glimpse of both the virtues and the vices of the African-American middle class," wrote the *New York Times* Book Review. It proved to be a bestseller and led to the publication of a collection of West's short stories and reminiscences called *The Richer, The Poorer*. Oprah Winfrey produced a TV miniseries on *The Wedding*.

At her death, in 1998, West was one of the last surviving members of the Harlem Renaissance. Dorothy West, an iconic Vineyarder, novelist, short story writer, editor and journalist, was truly an Island character.

***

Many more people deserve recognition. Judge Herbert Tucker (1915–2007) served as presiding judge of Dukes County from 1979 to 1985. Joseph Carter served as Oak Bluffs chief of police from 1998 to 2003 and is currently adjutant general of the Massachusetts National Guard. And there are many more important, impressive teachers, nurses, businessmen, housekeepers and laborers who deserve commendation for their efforts to make the Vineyard a better place for everyone.

EPILOGUE

In weaving the various strands into this tapestry, it is a challenge to make the finished product smooth and neat. There are loose ends to be tucked in. And because the tapestry is so broad, encompassing year-round Vineyarders, summer people and tourists, the overlap and missing threads are evident. The scourge of slavery, replaced by segregation and further demeaned by racism, is now an issue of class. And the experience of African Americans on Martha's Vineyard is a microcosm of the struggles of the nation as a whole.

When my wife Joyce and I drove to New Orleans to visit daughters Amy and Jill, we found ourselves on a mini–civil rights trip. Antietam, the bloodiest one-day battle not only of the Civil War but of all American history, proved a sobering step in freeing the slaves. A tour by a deacon of the Sixteenth Street Baptist Church in Birmingham brought home the sacrifices of the four girls killed in the 1963 bombing. A park adjacent to the church memorializes the harsh treatment of protesters by dogs, also in 1963. And in Jackson, Mississippi, we acknowledged where Medgar Evers was slain. It also was home to *The Help*, a novel about upper-class whites and their domestic blacks in the early 1960s. And, of course, New Orleans, particularly the Ninth Ward, is still rebuilding from Hurricane Katrina. Coming from Martha's Vineyard, we felt part of our country's crises and pain.

A *Boston Herald* article about the Vineyard, written in 1992 by DeWayne Wickham observed, "There is no segregated housing on Martha's Vineyard, except for a few enclaves of the very rich, where wealth, not color, restricts entry." Class structure, not skin color, separates people on the Vineyard.

People live together along the tight little streets of Martha's Vineyard without regard to the racial demons that haunt the rest of us. And in the evenings, as the summer heat gives way to the chilly night air, blacks and whites sit on their front porches and exchange greetings in an act of cordiality seldom seen on the American mainland. . . The civility of the people here is downright un-American.

The issue on the Vineyard is a difference in class based on income rather than race.

A tourist, and sometime vacationer, Diane Jones of Washington, D.C., offers her view of the Vineyard:

Initially, Martha's Vineyard was a place to visit in August. Specifically, it was a place to catch up with friends, take long walks and read books on the beach in the afternoon. A place for unexpected visits with friends who also happened to be on the island at the same time. A place to simply, and deeply, relax. The atmosphere and friendliness of people, summer visitors and residents alike, drew me back regularly. I knew African Americans had vacationed on the Vineyard for years, but only last year did I read about the history of African Americans on the island. That led to a wonderful tour of sites on the island with significance to the African American community. I am committed to learning more and doing what I can to support those who are telling the story about this special history.

And then there is the historical perspective, accomplished in a chat with longtime Oak Bluffs resident Bob Hughes.[65] At ninety-five, he has witnessed a great many changes on the Island yet doesn't feel it is that different from when he was a boy. In first grade, one of his twenty-five classmates was Dean Denniston. Bob said he never thought of Dean as being colored; he was just one of the kids. Shortly before the class was to graduate, now winnowed to eight students, they took a trip to Washington, D.C. Dean was informed that he could not stay in the hotel with the class in New York City because he was black. He refused and stayed the night in Bob Hughes's room. Of Oscar Denniston, Dean's father, Bob, said that he was a very good orator "but being colored held him back." During the summer, Bob explained, the Bradley Mission expanded into the old vaudeville theatre on Circuit Avenue and then retreated to the Masonic Avenue site in the off-season.

Bob recalled other African Americans on the Vineyard. Ambler Wormley ran the garage now owned by Michael DeBettencourt. Mr. Wormley lived on Uncas Avenue, across from Western Auto. George Frye's cobbler shop was on Circuit Avenue. "He was a good man," said Bob. "Passed the business to his son Buster. And his grandson, Vincent Frye, was quite a photographer, down in New York City. Still around."

Years ago, Bob delivered ice cream in a tub of ice to Pollard's Dining Room, near the Baptist Tabernacle. "His son, Albert Pollard, played the piano down at the movie theater. That was when we had the silent films. And when the Indians raced across the screen, Albert would pound that piano with all his might."

When he delivered ice cream to Shearer Cottage, Bob recalled "the old man," Charles Shearer. He had no recollection of a third child, just the two daughters, Lily and Sadie. Lily's husband, Lincoln Pope, "was a very good tennis player." Bob also recalled the Open Door as a club for African Americans, a home away from home for servants in the 1940s and 1950s. Bob has so many memories, now treasured in his recollections of the past.

Vineyarders may be ignorant of travesties endured by previous generations of African Americans. Yet those who have experienced the humiliation of racism or savored the exultation of new opportunities appreciate that the Vineyard offers an atmosphere that thrives on equality and acceptance. People on the Vineyard recognize that differences are to be extolled rather than condemned.

More can be said about the vibrant African American community on Martha's Vineyard. Many unrecognized people go about their daily lives not worrying about anything beyond their weekly paycheck. Yet all are integral threads in the fabric of the Vineyard. We recognize the actors, bus drivers, carpenters, civil servants, cooks, fishermen, hairdressers, housecleaners, landscapers, nurses and nursing assistants, policemen, store clerks, teachers, town employees and writers who contribute so much to the Island. African Americans serve as executive directors, elected officials and leaders of the business and political community. And we are proud to have the first African American to be elected president of the United States choose to vacation on Martha's Vineyard. That says it all.

The African American community, in 2010, has undergone many challenges and is now better suited to fit smoothly into the twenty-first century. We recognize and appreciate all it was, all it is and all it can be.

***

You come once, if you don't like it, you don't come back. Come twice, and you're hooked for life.
—*Dorothy West*

NOTES

PREFACE

1. Four fine books were published in 2005 that explore the African American experience on the Vineyard: Robert Hayden's *African Americans on Martha's Vineyard* profiles many prominent African Americans; Linsey Lee published the second volume of her interviews with senior Vineyarders, *More Vineyard Voices*, which captures memories of the twentieth century; Jill Nelson wrote *Finding Martha's Vineyard*, a memoir of her experience on the Island, with historical perspective and significant community leaders; and Dr. Elaine Cawley Weintraub wrote *Lighting the Trail* about her high school program, known as the African American Heritage Trail on Martha's Vineyard.

CHAPTER 1

2. A year later, the *Cerberus* itself was set afire by its own crew and sunk in Narragansett Bay to avoid capture by the French. The remains are a relic with the National Register of Historic Places in Rhode Island.
3. Research notes of R. Andrew Pierce on the genealogical records of Gay Head; used with permission. His upcoming book is titled *Wampanoag Families of Martha's Vineyard*.
4. Bob Woodruff is an amateur geologist and former director of the Vineyard Conservation Society. He explained that the clay on the cliffs dates back

100 million years, while the Vineyard itself is only about 1 million years old. Originally, the red clay of the cliffs was part of the Appalachian Mountains. It was ground down by the glacier, which squished the clay, enfolded it, inverted it and pushed it across Buzzard's Bay to the terminal moraine on the Vineyard. Bob Woodruff is an excellent resource for research papers, according to his grandson, Kyle. We agree.

5. R. Andrew Pierce, "Sharper Michael, Born a Slave, First Islander Killed in the Revolution," *Dukes County Intelligencer*, published by the Martha's Vineyard Museum, May 2005.

6. Jacqueline Holland, "The African American Presence on Martha's Vineyard," *Dukes County Intelligencer*, published by the Martha's Vineyard Museum, August, 1991.

7. Housed at the Falmouth Historical Society in Falmouth, MA. Appreciation extended to Mary Sicchio.

8. Levi Lincoln was a Minuteman during the Revolution and served his country well. In Worcester County, he was the clerk of court and probate judge; he was elected to the Massachusetts legislature and appointed attorney general by President Jefferson. He was elected lieutenant governor and then succeeded to governor of Massachusetts. His two sons also served as governors. And he was the author's great-great-great-great-grandfather.

CHAPTER 2

9. Jeremiah Pease, "Diary of Jeremiah Pease," *Dukes County Intelligencer*, published by Martha's Vineyard Museum, November 1980.

10. Saunders apprenticed his son, also John, to Melatiah Pease on January 1, 1793, for seventeen years, perhaps as a form of protection against the vagaries of being an African American. John Saunders Jr. became rather "well known for his great strength and as a singer and dancer," according to the *Vineyard Gazette*, August 11, 1876. Priscilla Freeman owned land on the shore of Tisbury Great Pond and, in the mid-1800s, petitioned for riparian rights (shoreline access) as a landowner, which she felt she had been denied, perhaps because of her color. In the same article, it was noted that "her sweet toned voice is often heard in prayer and conference meetings."

11. Pierce, research and notes.

12. Ibid.

13. *Falmouth Enterprise*, May 14, 1976.
14. Ibid.
15. Eighteen months earlier, the town council in Judystown, Pennsylvania, challenged Gould because of his fiery abolitionist rhetoric to a mostly African American audience. His speech was "exciting the colored population of this borough." The council requested he "desist from his efforts." *Liberator*, February 13, 1836.
16. Carter Woodson, ed., *The Journal of Negro History* (Washington, D.C.: Association for the Study of Negro Life and History, 1919).
17. Linsey Lee, interview with Captain Charles Vanderhoop Jr., 2000, in *More Vineyard Voices*, 114.
18. The story of an escaped slave was told in elaborate detail in the *Vineyard Gazette* of February 3, 1921, recounted by Netta Vanderhoop, about her grandmother Beulah.

CHAPTER 3

19. Grover, *Fugitive's Gibraltar*, 287.
20. Williamston, North Carolina, figures in our story again, more than a century later, in 1964, during the height of the civil rights movement.
21. *Falmouth Enterprise*, February 6, 1981.

CHAPTER 4

22. Richard Miller, "Two Vineyard 'Men of Color' Who Fought in the Civil War," *Dukes County Intelligencer*, published by the Martha's Vineyard Museum, 1994, 28.
23. Ibid., 41.
24. *Martha's Vineyard Herald*, July 13, 1889.
25. Chris Baer, "A Hole in the Bible," *Dukes County Intelligencer*, published by the Martha's Vineyard Museum, Autumn 2009.
26. Erich Luening, "Scouring the Seas…Race and the Black Whaling Captains of American History," *USARiseUp. USARiseUp* is a digital offspring of *RiseUp*, an online magazine on race, November 30, 2009.
27. *Vineyard Gazette* obituary, September 12, 1907.
28. "African American Whaling Captain; Notes for Bibliophiles," Special Collections, Providence Public Library, October 9, 2009.

29. American Indian News Service: Smithsonian National Museum of the American Indian. Interviewed at the Smithsonian. Penny Gamble-Williams, the former Sunksqua, or female sachem, of the Chappaquiddick Band of the Wampanoag Nation of Massachusetts, shared her experiences with the American Indian News Service, October 17, 2009.

CHAPTER 5

30. Railton, *History of Martha's Vineyard*, 417–19.
31. Linsey Lee, interview with Dean Denniston, 1996, in *Vineyard Voices*, 162.
32. The Baptist Temple no longer stands. It was constructed in 1877, two years prior to the wrought-iron Methodist Tabernacle at Wesleyan Grove Campground, which is still extant.
33. Holland, "African American Presence on Martha's Vineyard."
34. Linsey Lee, interview with Doris Pope Jackson, 1996, in *More Vineyard Voices*, 132.
35. Adelaide Cromwell, "History of Oak Bluffs as a Popular Resort for Blacks," *Dukes County Intelligencer*, published by the Martha's Vineyard Museum, 1984, 15.
36. Jackson interview, *More Vineyard Voices*, 131.
37. Russell, *Profile of a Black Heritage*, 37.
38. Denniston interview, *Vineyard Voices*, 166.
39. *Boston Globe*, April 8, 2006.
40. *Vineyard Gazette*, August 8, 1986.
41. Jackson interview, *More Vineyard Voices*, 131.

CHAPTER 6

42. Cromwell, "History of Oak Bluffs."
43. Holland, "African American Presence on Martha's Vineyard."
44. *Vineyard Gazette*, August 13, 1948.
45. Railton, *History of Martha's Vineyard*, 407.
46. *Vineyard Gazette*, "Fond Memories of a Black Childhood," June 25, 1971.
47. Linsey Lee, interview with Barbara Townes, 1983, in *More Vineyard Voices*, 148.
48. *Vineyard Gazette*, January 18, 1957.

49. Olive Tomlinson's (unpublished) memoirs, which she defines as "an episodic grasp of reality," 45.
50. Railton, *History of Martha's Vineyard*, 377, 379–81.
51. Cromwell, "History of Oak Bluffs."
52. J. Riche Coleman, "Being Black in Old Oak Bluffs," *Vineyard Gazette*, August 20, 1971.
53. Linsey Lee, interview with Joseph Stiles, 2002, in *More Vineyard Voices*, 59.
54. Townes interview, *More Vineyard Voices*.
55. Linsey Lee, interview with Dorothy West, 1983, in *Vineyard Voices*.

Chapter 7

56. Durr (wife of Clifford Durr), *Outside the Magic Circle*, 281.
57. Bausum, *Freedom Riders*, 7.

Chapter 8

58. Linsey Lee, interview with Nancy Whiting, 1993, in *Vineyard Voices*, 54.
59. *Vineyard Gazette*, January 22, 1993.
60. Hayden, *African Americans on Martha's Vineyard*, 201.

Chapter 11

61. *New York Times*, August 16, 2009.
62. *Cape Cod Online*, August 25, 2009.

Chapter 12

63. *Martha's Vineyard Times*, August 20, 2009.
64. Holland, "African American Presence on Martha's Vineyard," 20.

Epilogue

65. Bob Hughes interview, April 8, 2010, in Oak Bluffs.

BIBLIOGRAPHY

Banks, Charles. *History of Martha's Vineyard*. Edgartown, MA: Martha's Vineyard Historical Society, 1911.

Bausum, Ann. *The Freedom Riders: John Lewis and Jim Zwerg on the Front Lines of the Civil Rights Movement*. Washington, D.C.: National Geographic Society, 2006.

Cromwell, Adelaide M. *Unveiled Voices Unvarnished Memories*. Columbia: University of Missouri Press, 2007.

Durr, Virginia. *Outside the Magic Circle*. Tuscaloosa: University of Alabama, 1985.

Grover, Kathryn. *The Fugitive's Gibraltar*. Amherst: University of Massachusetts Press, 2001.

Hayden, Robert. *African Americans on Martha's Vineyard*. Boston: Select Publications, 2005.

Lee, Linsey. *More Vineyard Voices*. Edgartown, MA: Martha's Vineyard Historical Society, 2005.

———. *Vineyard Voices*. Edgartown, MA: Martha's Vineyard Historical Society, 1998.

Nelson, Jill. *Finding Martha's Vineyard*. New York: Random House, 2005.

Railton, Arthur. *History of Martha's Vineyard*. Beverly, MA: Commonwealth Editions, 2006.

Russell, Dr. Lester. *Profile of a Black Heritage*. New York, 1977.

Salmond, John. *The Conscience of a Lawyer*. Tuscaloosa: University of Alabama Press, 1990.

Snodgrass, Mary. *The Underground Railroad*. Armonk, NY: Sharpe Reference, 2008.

Weintraub, Elaine Cawley. *Lighting the Trail*. N.p.: Massachusetts Foundation for the Humanities, 2005.

West, Dorothy. *The Dorothy West Martha's Vineyard*. Jefferson, NC: McFarland & Company, 2001.

ABOUT THE AUTHOR

After a stint as an elementary schoolteacher and a couple of decades as a nursing home administrator, Tom Dresser realized he wanted to write. Besides freelance contributions to the local press, he has self-published five booklets based on favorite New England areas and printed two books on demand. In 2008, The History Press published *Mystery on the Vineyard*, which went into a second printing. For more information, visit thomasdresser.com.

When Tom attended his thirtieth high school reunion, he ran into a former classmate who invited him down to Martha's Vineyard for a weekend, and the rest, as they say, is history. Tom and Joyce have been married a dozen years.

Tom has two daughters, both in education. Amy Dresser Held (spouse: Brian) works in Los Angeles, and Jill Dresser teaches in New Orleans. He has three stepchildren—Jeremy Jones (spouse: Annie), Jennifer Jones Smyth (spouse: Pete) and Christopher Jones (spouse: Raisa)—and three grandchildren: Shealyn Heather Smyth, Molly Rose Held and Dylan Thomas Held.

Other Books by Thomas Dresser
thomasdresser.com

Dogtown: A Village Lost in Time, 1995
Beyond Bar Harbor, 1996
It Happened In Haverhill, 1997
Looking at Lawrence, 1997
Tommy's Tour of the Vineyard, 2005
Mystery on the Vineyard (The History Press), 2008
In My Life (fiction), 2009
It Was 40 Years Ago Today, 2009